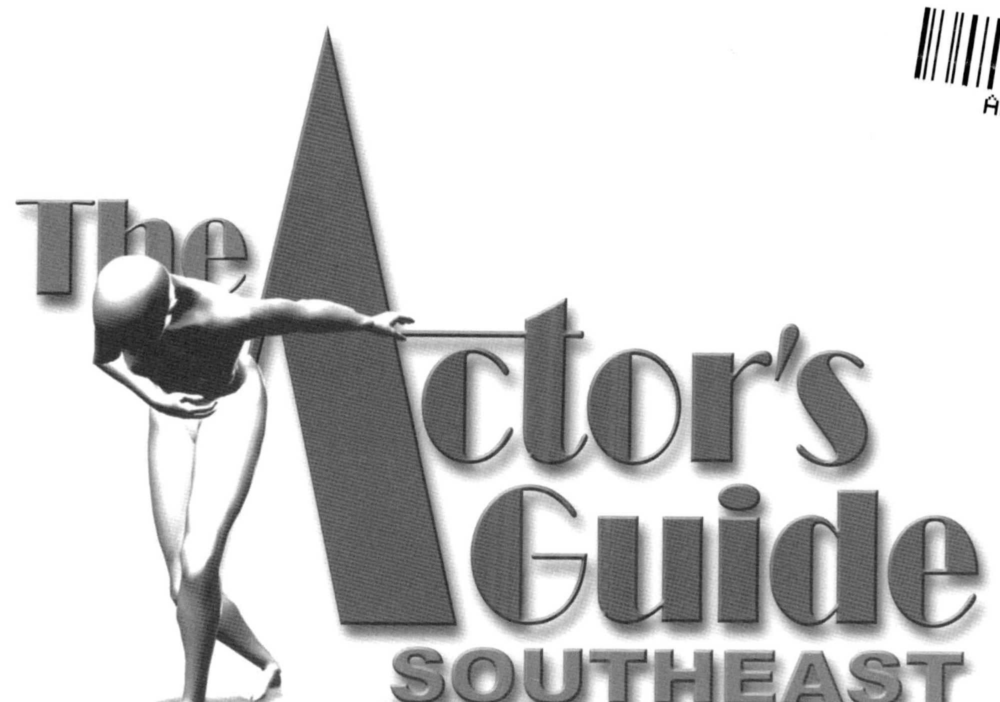

An Introduction to the Regional Film & Television Market

BY NAN MCELROY & MELISSA OHLMAN-ROBERGE

Published by:

Illustrata, Inc.
Atlanta, GA

800.594.3457

For complete ordering information,
call the above number or see:

theactorsguide.com

First printing second edition 2001
First printing first edition 1997

Printed in the United States of America

Table of Contents

Foreword

by Steve Coulter

Hopefully, you just bought this book. Perhaps you haven't yet — you're still sitting there cross-legged on the floor of your favorite mega-chain bookstore, nestled cozily between Theatre Arts and New Age Healing & Nutrition. Just get up, hobble over to the cash register and buy the darn thing.

If you're an actor living in the Southeast, you need this book: simple as that. I bought it myself when I decided to focus a bit more on doing voice-over work. That chapter alone saved me about two weeks and fourteen phone calls. I still refer to various directory listings several times a month, and when as a director and instructor I get calls from actors with questions about the business, I find myself saying time and time again, "Well, there's this book…"

Acting is a very difficult business to pursue. You need tools that you can trust to help in that pursuit: this book is one of those tools. The information here can help you figure out how to make a career of this acting thing — literally saving you months, if not years of frustration, especially if you are just starting out. You can find the current address of that casting director in Alabama, the name of a good photographer who won't steal your money and actually take pictures that look like you, or what steps to follow in finding an agent (or getting a better one). If you are already enjoying a career as an actor here and are mulling over a move to New York or Los Angeles, you might want to take a look at that chapter of the book before you pack your bags (it could save you one or two nasty surprises). The individuals quoted on these pages are professionals — they make a living doing the stuff they are talking about. It's what you call good old-fashioned wisdom, so you might want to listen to it.

But all the terrific information and guidance in this book are useless to you if you're not also out there working to be a better actor (which the book actually encourages you to do). Learning the business of acting before learning the craft of acting is putting that ol' cart before the horse. Once while shooting a TV movie I was approached by a young lady who had about three lines in an upcoming scene with me. While we were waiting for the set to be lit, she picked my brain about who the best agents were, how to get in to see a certain casting director, which photographers I'd recommend for her new pictures, etc. Then, when the director called us over to the set, this young actor turned to me and asked, "Do you have the sides for this scene?" She had known she had these three lines for over five weeks, and she DIDN'T KNOW HER LINES!! She was on her way to being one fine networker, but she was also more than well on her way to being a lousy actor.

So...read this book and then go act. Find a theatre company that is doing the kind of plays you want to do and audition for them. Or find a class you like and start taking it. Write a play, borrow money from your Aunt Lulu and rent a theatre space to perform it in. Get together with some fellow actors and read Sam Shepard plays together in someone's living room. The more you act, the better you will get. The better you get, the more joy will get doing it. And you will want to keep on doing it so you can feel more of that joy.

One word about the woman who originated this guide. I've known Nan McElroy for over ten years now. I have acted with her, I've directed her, I've coveted her flourishing voice-over career, and I have enjoyed her friendship. She is also an accomplished Avid editor (I trusted her to edit my film, which is something akin to trusting her to deliver my child), and she found some time in there to become fluent in Italian. She does many things and she Does Them All Very Well. She and her co-author Melissa Ohlman-Roberge have put together a straight-forward, no-nonsense, terrifically useful book. So, if you're still sitting on the floor of that bookstore, get up and go buy it. While you're at it, buy your Mom a nice card.

Oh, and don't forget to learn your lines.

Steve Coulter is an Atlanta-based actor and director who has worked extensively in theatres across the U.S., including the Guthrie Theatre, the Alliance Theatre, the Berkshire Theatre Festival, and Musical Theatreworks in NY. He has appeared in over a dozen films, including A Time to Kill, Eddie, Chill Factor, and Letters From a Wayward Son. His television credits include Another World, Andersonville, In the Heat of the Night, and two seasons on I'll Fly Away. He has studied with Rosemary Harris, Eric Morris, at the Actors Studio in NY, and is a graduate of the North Carolina School of the Arts. He has taught the Scene Study and Text Analysis workshops at the IMAGE Film & Video Center for over 8 years, and recently wrote and directed the short film The Etiquette Man, which is at this printing enjoying a very successful festival run.

Are you...

...someone with no professional experience, curious about what it takes to work as an on-camera actor in the southeastern United States? Or an actor with a theatrical background who would like to cross over and pursue work in film and television? An experienced actor coming from another part of the country seeking information about the southeastern market? Then this publication has been written with you in mind. Nowhere is there as concise or complete a compilation of the information you need to pursue work as an actor in the Southeast region.

One of the difficulties in getting started in this business is simply learning the ropes: what you need, what is expected of you, who's who, what they can and can't do for you, etc. Frankly, there a great many people who have this knowledge. But separating facts from hearsay, finding those individuals who can really help you, and then convincing them to mentor you in the basics can almost be a career in itself.

We wanted to create the kind of how-to manual we wish we'd had when beginning our careers — one that would serve as a realistic introduction for newcomers, as well as an orientation for theatre and relocating actors.

In addition, we've included a companion regional industry directory that can be replaced as updates become available.

Of course, due to the nature of the industry we cannot guarantee complete accuracy, but we have made every attempt to verify any information we include. We also post updates as we become aware of them on our web site theactorsguide.com, where we hope all listings will soon be available online.

For the second edition, we conducted numerous interviews with a variety of professionals who live and work throughout the region. Without exception, they were extremely forthcoming with comments and opinions, contributing a great deal of personal insight into the particular workings of the business. There's also information on the effect of the digital revolution, and an update on the regional independent film market. Additionally we've included an entire chapter on maintaining your sanity and integrity while working in a profession whose success depends so much on how others perceive you.

One last note. This manual is a product of experience — ours, and other professionals we've known. It is *not* the last word. There are few hard and fast rules in this business. If there were, somebody would have written that book a long time ago. The final word will in fact be yours, and will depend on how and why you look to work as an actor. If **The Actor's Guide** assists you in that quest, then we have fulfilled our mission.

The following individuals are friends, colleagues and professionals (not to mention relatives) who volunteered their support in every way to help us make this as reliable and credible a publication as possible. We know they all have demands on their time and we would like to acknowledge their generosity in returning our phone calls, reviewing our drafts, giving detailed comments and feedback, offering advice and encouragement, and in general lending the kind of support we needed to make this a truly helpful publication. Carol Bacall, Della Cole, Meredith Folland, Nancy Gable, Pride Chamberlain, Lisa France, Henderson Gilleland, Pam Glotzbach, Marian Guyot, Annie Harvey, Jerry Immel, Carol Jones, Dick Klinger, Dee Knapp, John Knapp, My Dad H. A. McElroy, Margo Moorer, Dean Taylor, Rusty Wiggs, Libby Wittermore.

Paul Armbruster is a voice-over actor with over twenty years performing/teaching experience in Los Angeles, New York, and Atlanta. He has taught voice-over for both L. A. Broadcasters and the Alliance Theatre.

Sandi Bell had been an agent for over 15 years, starting in Miami, moving to Los Angeles, then returning to Orlando in 1995. She's the only totally exclusive agent in the Central Florida region, working mainly in film, television and commercials.

Rona Burns is the agent/owner of the Burns Agency. After fifteen years in Atlanta, she recently returned to open an office in North Carolina (her home state) while continuing to maintain an Atlanta presence. "It's a new beginning that's optimistic," said Rona.

Diana Cardéa (Contributor, *You Should Do Voice-over*) is one of the top voice-over talents in the Southeast region.

Ken Carpenter is a writer/producer/director based in Nashville. Credits include the hour dramatic pilot *The Sullivan Sisters* for PAX TV; he currently has several film and television projects in development.

Jill Jane Clements has been acting and directing for over twenty years. Favorite roles include Lenny in *Crimes of the Heart*, Miranda in *A Hole in the Dark* and Mrs. Candor in *The School for Scandal*. She directed *Tru* for Theatre in the Square and *Our Town* for the Theatrical Outfit. Film credits include *My Cousin Vinny*, *The Real McCoy* and various characters on In the *Heat of the Night*. She is always, she says, looking for work.

Judy Simpson Cook was a talent agent with JTA, Inc. in Charlotte for 15 years until May 2000, when she left to become a fulltime actor and playwright. She has performed on stage and film.

Stuart Culpepper is an accomplished theatre and film actor and a staple in the national voice-over market. He lives, works (and enjoys spending lots of time with his grandson) in Atlanta.

Traci Danielle is the owner and senior agent at Brevard Talent Group, which represents actors for film, television and commercials in the Central Florida market. The agency is franchised by SAG/AFTRA/AEA.

Jim Donadio enters the 29th year of his professional career as an actor, director, fight choreographer, teacher, producer, and screenwriter for stage and screen. He has criss-crossed the country putting together an extensive repertory resume, and is now grateful to no longer have to live out of two suitcases.

Randall Edwards (Contributor, *Mini Modeling Intro*) has been an agent since 1987, working in Florida for much of that time. Currently he is a senior agent at Atlanta Models & Talent, the oldest agency in the South.

Shannon Eubanks, now in Atlanta, continues a quarter-century career as an actress, director, playwright, screenwriter, and acting teacher. Hang in there long enough and you'll no longer have to have a "real" job either.

Fincannon and Associates. Mark, Lisa Mae and Craig Fincannon began casting over twenty years ago, moving from Charlotte to Wilmington in 1985. Credits include the Emmy-winning *From the Earth to the Moon*, along with over 100 hours of feature film credits, 10 mini-series and 200 hours of episodic television.

Wilbur Fitzgerald has been an actor in film and voice-over for the over 20 years. He now works primarily out of New York and Atlanta. His work for NBC, Showtime, CTV Newsnet, and many commercial clients can be heard at voboy.com.

Michael Fulmer had a successful career in retail advertising (Macy's, Art Coordinator for the Atlanta Journal Constitution) before moving back to Birmingham in 1987 to open Real People Models & Talent. Fourteen years later, it's the largest agency in the state.

Tammy Green and her sister are the owners of The Green Agency in Miami Beach, a SAG-franchised agency that represents children to seniors who have international, national and regional production credits. The agency and its staff have over 50 years combined booking and management experience.

Kay Butler Hallahan (Contributor, *California Dreamin'*) is the owner of Talent Resources talent consultation. Her experience in the industry spans over twenty years and includes divese aspects of the business such as talent agent, advertising industry art director, and writer. Known for her expertise on SAG and AFTRA commercial and industrial contracts, she also leads workshops for producers and directors on the same subject.

Kathy Hardegree is President of Atlanta Models & Talent, celebrating her 30th anniversary with the company in July of 2000. As a talent agent she represents actors, voice-over talent, and models for television, radio, feature films, industrial films and advertising print throughout the United States.

Sylvia Harmon has been a professional actress for over 35 years, appearing in New York, Los Angeles, regional theatres across the country as well as extensively in film and television. She is the owner and instructor of The Actor's Place in Virginia Beach, celebrating it's tenth anniversary in 2001.

Linda Higgs has been in the entertainment field for over nine years as an actor, a manager/talent agent at a Nashville union agency, and finally as a talent coordinator and casting director. She is currently in partnership with Regina Moore completing the casting team of Moore-Higgs Casting in Nashville.

Tommy Housworth is an Atlanta actor/writer, with numerous film, commercial, and industrial credits. He teaches acting and improv at the Alliance Theatre and The Company Acting Studio. He is the director of 7 Course Theatre, which provides entertainment for corporate events.

Paige Johnston and Mitzi Corrigan founded Corrigan & Johnston Casting in Charlotte in 1996 after working freelance for several years. Their Film Division, Commercial Division and Extras Division are dedicated to providing clients with the best in casting resources and services.

Jen Kelley began her career in Los Angeles in 1992 as a children's talent agent, co-founding the successful youth division of Talent Group, Inc. She is currently an agent for both children and adults at People Store in Atlanta, and is the co-author (with Brenda Krochmal) of **The Actor s Guide for Kids**.

Tracy Kilpatrick runs The Casting Office in her home state of North Carolina, in Wilmington. For over eight years she's cast everything from features to photo shoots, and loves the variety of locations where projects take her. Credits include *Songcatcher, Dead Man Walking* and *Forrest Gump,* among others.

Rebecca Koon has an MA in Acting from USC, Columbia and has worked on stage and before the camera for over 20 years. Based in Charlotte, NC she has a husband, child and pets to enrich as well as complicate life.

Brenda Krochmal is a veteran teacher with over 20 years experience. She has taught theater classes for children, prepared them for Broadway showcases and spent countless hours on the set with her actress-daughter, Jenny. Brenda is the co-author of the **Actor's Guide for Kids** with Jen Kelley.

Terry Loughlin's credits include *A Time To Kill, October Sky, Chill Factor, Billy Bathgate,* and *Simple Twist of Fate,* numerous TV movies and recurring roles on *Matlock, In the Heat of the Night,* and *Savannah.* He is currently Resident Director of Charlotte Repertory Theatre, and spends his summers directing for The Flat Rock Playhouse.

Lisina Longo is a native New Yorker trained professionally at The Stella Adler Conservatory, The New York School of Performing Arts and Boston University. She is the founder and owner of The Company Acting Studio in Atlanta.

Carl McIntyre continues to live in Charlotte, NC and work throughout the Southeast or where ever they'll hire him. He has a wonderful life with his wife Elizabeth and his two daughters, Grace and Liza.

Jimmi McCarter was former member of Dean Martin's "Golddiggers" starring for two years in their syndicated show, a principal in numerous national commercials and a former recording artist for Warner Bros. Records in Nashville before she became the owner/agent at The Cannon Group talent agency there.

Roxanne McMillan is the owner of RTA in North Miami. She got her bug for the business in the late 70's working for Ruth Foreman, the "First Lady of Theatre." Through lots of work and determination she's been fulfilling her own dreams ever since by helping talented people find employment.

Regina Moore began her career over 22 years ago as an actor and eventually moved into production. She has owned and operated a talent supplies and service business, served as editor of the Talent Reporter and held instructional workshops along with Linda Higgs, her co-founder of Moore-Higgs Casting in Nashville.

Kimberly Mullen began her work in casting in 1992 as Mel Johnson's associate in Orlando, and also as Casting Department Head for Nickelodeon. She founded Kimberly Mullen Casting (along with casting husband Mark Mullen) in 1999, now located at Universal Studios in Orlando.

Bob Newcomb's work as a director/cameraman in commercials spans thirty years, and continues through relationships with several production companies around the country. He is a multiple Clio, Addy, One Show ward winner and has sever times appeared on the Ad Age Best 100 list.

Linda Newcomb has worked in the talent business as an agent, casting director and teacher for over thirty years. She is a full time talent representative in Charlotte, NC with JTA, the company that launched her career in 1970.

Bill Nunn first gained national attention for his portrayal of Radio Raheem in Spike Lee's *Do the Right Thing,* also starring in Lee's *He Got Game, School Daze* and *Mo' Better Blues.* He's also familiar to film audiences as a cop keeping Whoopi Goldberg undercover in *Sister Act,* and Harrison Ford's physical therapist in *Regarding Henry.* His extensive stage work includes roles in *Fences, A Soldier's Play, MacBeth* and *Blues for an Alabama Sky,* in addition to directing numerous children's theatre productions and developing a comedy act with longtime friend Al Cooper in the early 80's.

Robin O'Dell lives in Tampa and has performed professionally in films, television and theatre throughout the Southeast for over 12 years. Highlights include the *The First of May* with Julie Harris, *The Runaway* with Maya Angelou, and episodes of *ER, Dawson's Creek,*

From the Earth to the Moon and a recurring role opposite Corbin Bernsen on *The Cape.*

Afemo Omilami's extensive resume includes regional and Broadway stage work, film credits of *The Firm, Remember the Titans* and *Forrest Gump,* as well as a variety of TV movies and episodics.

Elisabeth Omilami's versatility as an actress spans stage, film, television, commercial and voice-over work. Notable appearances include *Selma, Lord Selma, The Perfect Crime* and *A Time to Kill.* Afemo and Elisabeth both live and work out of Atlanta.

Kathy Payne is an veteran Atlanta-based film, television, and commercial actress and voice-talent.

Rodney Pickel is a professional actor and drama instructor living in Nashville, TN. His credits include commercials, short and feature films, and numerous stage productions.

Mike Pniewski is a L.A. native and successful character actor in commercials, film and series television for over 16 years. His training includes a B.A. at UCLA, the famous Groundling Theatre in Hollywood and cold reading studies with Brian Reise. Mike teaches a variety of classes through The Company Acting Studio in Atlanta.

Jacqueline G. Pressley established Capital Artists of North Carolina in 1992 to represent professional actors throughout the US, with emphasis in the Southeast with offices in Raleigh-Durham and Wilmington.

Rebecca Shrager is the owner of People Store, Inc. which has been supplying talent for major film & television projects in the Southeast and across the country for over seventeen years.

Annette Stilwell has been casting commercials and industrials in Atlanta for over twenty years.

Judith Sullivan brings to her clients an unusually rich combination of training and experience in both professional and personal voice/speech proficiency. She is one of Atlanta's top voice talents and has been featured in hundreds of radio and TV commercials as well as industrials and major motion pictures.

Sally Vaughan has been a copywriter, producer, sales rep, creative services director, casting director and talent agent over the past 25 years. (Consequently, she feels she has earned every wrinkle on her face.) She is currently the VO and industrial agent at People Store in Atlanta.

Danny Vinson has been acting professionally for six years, with a range of credits including feature films, national commercials and print, industrial, and coaching workshops. He lives in Nashville, TN.

Rebecca Wackler, formerly of Atlanta, is an acting coach, director, playwright, actor and personal trainer living in Los Angeles.

Juanell Walker and Charlotte Dennison are owners of Talent Trek Agency (SAG), established in 1983. With four regional offices and the main one in Knoxville, they work with casting directors and production companies supplying talent needs for music videos, television, industrials, radio and films.

Jeff Winter has a uniquely familiar voice-over style that most people have heard on national commercials for many years. He considers himself a "working voice," rounding out a full time career, voicing promos, narrating documentaries, corporate/industrial and interactive pieces.

Marsha Wulf is the founder of TalentLink, Inc., a full service agency representing experienced actors, principally serving Virginia, D.C., Maryland, Penn. and North Carolina. She holds a Bachelor of Arts in Theater, has more than eight years experience as a writer and producer for CBS and ABC affiliates.

Lori Wyman was an agent in Miami for five years before she began casting over twenty years ago (*Miami Vice* is an early credit). Other credits include film, television and, she estimates, over 1000 commercials.

Getting the Picture

You must have talent, skill, discipline and patience.
Anyone who doesn't will sooner or later be weeded out.

Marsha Wulf, Owner/Agent
TalentLink, Inc.

If It's Too Good To Be True...

You're scanning through the Sunday want ads and you see an ad you've seen before:

ACTORS/MODELS

Now casting major independent film

All types — No experience necessary

Call for appointment

Sounds exciting, doesn't it? "I've always wondered...." You call. Sure enough, no experience required. They're looking for new faces. They'd like to see you. You set up an interview, and you go. You're a little nervous, but the man with whom you have the appointment makes you feel very comfortable. He jokes with you, tells you about his agency, all the work they've done, who they've represented and how successful their clients are (there are headshots all over the walls!), and to you, having no reference point, it all sounds swell...JUST WHAT YOU WANTED TO HEAR.

Now this man can't promise anything of course, but he thinks you just may have something, you know, something that would be worth your giving it a shot. But *if* you're selected (they have several other candidates) you'll need training to compensate for your lack of experience. And this "agency" just happens to offer the very best training available. And headshots, why, they have an excellent photographer as well, right on staff. And some professional make-up. And of course, there's a small application fee. All you have to do is write us a check for $500. Or $800. Or $1000. Or more. They even have a payment plan.

Get the picture?

This is the way these so-called "agents" make their money — by taking advantage of hopeful individuals whose lack of experience makes them prime candidates for exploitation. "It just breaks my heart to hear about people who just hand over money because they hear the promise of work," laments veteran actor Jill Jane Clements.

The normal process is this: a talent agent is contacted by a producer or casting director with descriptions of the roles to be cast. The agent calls actors they represent to audition for those roles. If the actor is cast, the agent earns a commission when and only when the actor is paid.

The bottom line?

Never purchase anything as a condition of representation.

Never pay to be represented.

It is never necessary to pay for an opportunity or an interview.

A LEGITIMATE TALENT AGENT MAKES MONEY WHEN YOU DO AND AT NO OTHER TIME.

Period. End of lecture.

For in depth information on common scams, how to avoid them and how to take care yourself in the process, we recommend **The Glam Scam** by Erik Flowers.

Realities & Expectations

Acting is an art, a craft and a passion. The production of commercials, film and television is a business — don't ever forget it.

In order to get the opportunity to practice your art, you need to understand the business. It's also important that you understand the product you are trying to sell: YOU. Your ability, your look, your personality, and everything that is unique and special about you. You have an individual and personal appeal and it's up to you to identify it. If you can't, then you can bet no one else will be able to either.

First Things First

Start by identifying for yourself why you are considering acting as a career. An actor is not something you decide to be. It is something that on some level you already are, and the decision comes into play when you evaluate how and to what degree to integrate it into your life. How much time are you willing and able devote to earning the craft? To understanding the business? To the development of the required professional and admilistrative skills you'll need (you'll be self-employed, you know)? We are constantly approached by newcomers who ask, "Everybody tells me I should be an actor. What should I do?" We're quite sure they mean well, but we should ask whether "everybody" knows anything about acting, the business or one iota about what is involved in even considering supporting yourself as an actor, because "everybody" will probably not be around two years and three jobs later when you ask yourself "WHAT WAS I THINKING?" If it is acting that you love, then you can find a place to do it. The challenge will be whether you can earn enough to support yourself.

Get a real job and forget about it.

Judy Cook, PLAYWRIGHT AND FORMER AGENT, JTA

I went into the casting office during a feature I was producing and I could not believe what I saw: there must've been (and I'm not exaggerating) 20,000 headshots, lying in piles all over the floor. Unbelievable! All of those talented people on the floor! All I could think was 'Thank God I do something other than act.'

Lisa France, ACTOR, INDIE FILMMAKER, NEW YORK

"The most successful actors are the ones who take themselves seriously both as artists and as business people,' says Rebecca Shrager, owner/agent at People Store in Atlanta. Approach your career as a professional. Set specific goals and take action to attain them. One of director George Watkins' favorite quotes is "Luck is the residue of design." Opportunities come about as the result of the time and effort you spend attempting to create them — sometimes directly, sometimes not.

When you represent yourself to people in the business, it should be in your best light. This includes not only producers, agents and casting directors but receptionists and other talent as well. We believe this ability comes from being as comfortable as possible with who you are and what you have to offer: as an actor (important) and as a human being (even more important). Avoid any gossip and negativity you encounter — and avoid generating it at all costs. It's destructive, serves no purpose, spreads like wildfire and is never something you'd want to be known for. "I've taken a lot of guff from a lot of people, and even bit my lip 'til it hurt because I know that anyone, anytime can be replaced with one phone call," says actor Danny Vinson.

A Los Angeles director-friend asks, "Why do you want to be an actor? It's the worst job in the world!" He's right; it can be grueling, thankless and downright demeaning. So it's tremendously important that if you want to pursue a career at which the odds of success are slim at best, you must

Shannon Eubanks tells the story of auditioning and even screentesting for a recurring role in a television series. Everyone agreed, this role was hers. Unbeknownst to her however, she bore a striking resemblance to the executive producer's ex-wife, to whom he was paying a hefty chunk of alimony. "I just can't look at that face every week," he said. She lost the job.

develop your own method of sustaining yourself mentally, emotionally and spiritually during the times when:

- you can't get an agent
- you can't get an audition
- you were getting auditions, now you're not, and no one will tell you why
- you always audition against one person in particular, who always gets booked instead of you
- your roommate has two auditions a day and you have two a month, or vice versa
- your first film audition is canceled after the eight hour drive to the audition, or the film role is written out
- your first film role is written out before your shoot date
- your first film role is edited out of the film

- you'd like more film work but can only seem to get commercial auditions
- you'd like more commercial work but can only get non-broadcast auditions
- you were hot and now you're not. "There have been times when I couldn't buy a part," adds actor/director/insturctor Terry Loughlin.

"But that's not fair!" you say. Well, that's really not the point. This is one business where it's crucial that you concentrate on the things you're able to control, and find a way to keep the rest of it from eating you alive.

For example, according to the Screen Actors Guild, there were 96,000 SAG members nationwide as of December 1999; at least half of those are in Los Angeles. Of those 96,000 SAG actors, historically 2 to 4% earn over 85% of all SAG income. Over 90% of all SAG actors earn $10,000 a year or less.

This estimate does not include the even larger number of non-union actors, which could easily be estimated at a ratio of ten to one. (Kay Butler Hallahan is a former agent and owner of Talent Resources in Atlanta. She calculates the ratio this way: when she goes to a local professional theatre, she contrasts the number headshots for non-union actors with the number of SAC/AFTRA actors.) A ten-to-one ratio would equate to yet another 960,000 actors looking for work.

In the face of statistics like these, your ability to survive and succeed in this business will have much less to do with what kind of actor you are than what kind of person you are.

Still interested? Well, of *course* you are... Read on.

Stuart Culpepper recalls that early on when he began enjoying some commercial success as a voice talent, he perhaps took it a bit for granted. During an Atlanta magazine interview he made the error of commenting that "the money's nice, but it's like prostituting my art." Youth. "I didn't work again for 2 years," he smiles. "Now I say that commercial work is God's way of subsidizing the American Theatre. And I mean it."

Opportunities

Almost everything produced by the film and video industry can be divided into three general categories:

- Television and Feature Film
- Commercials
- Non-Broadcast

You may pursue one or more of these areas, depending on your own interests and goals as an actor. "My feeling is that as a regional actor, to support yourself you need to be a threat in everything," says Charlotte-based actor Carl McIntyre.

Film and Television

In a secondary market like the Southeast, an actor on a film or television series is usually hired either weekly, as a **day-player** (a day at a time), or as an **extra**. (See the chapter on Training for a discussion of extra work.) Larger **principal** (speaking) roles are almost always cast out of Los Angeles or New York.

The number of films and television series being produced throughout the region varies quite a bit from year to year and state to state. Due to lucrative incentives and the benefit of the exchange rate, Canada has drawn a tremendous amount of film work away from the primary and secondary markets. However, all states in the region are making concerted efforts not only to promote themselves as locations, but in fostering the development of the industry itself, and many people are encouraged by the statistics and see a viable future for film here. Of course the number of factors involved in the

You can work here. You can breathe here. You can support your family here. You can build resumes and relationships here. You won't be discovered here.

MARSHA WULF
TALENTLINK, INC.

direction the industry takes are almost limitless, including everything from foreign incentives to the overall economy.

One change that has taken place over the last decade or so is the increase in the popularity and production of independent films. Nashville-based producer/director Ken Carpenter describes independent film spirit as "capturing the unique creative expression by each individual filmmaker." That, combined with the nuts-and-bolts definition offered by Lisa Fincannon: "any film for which there is no distribution deal." The independent budget is typically smaller (from several thousands to a few million), and the funding sources are as diverse as the films themselves.

Traditionally, the major portion of film production has been financed out of Los Angeles (a.k.a. the "Hollywood" film) and as such is dependent on its blessings and funding to ever have any hope of theatrical release. In the last decade however, a combination of factors has made the independent film a more viable alternative to its Hollywood counterpart. These include the periodic success of indie films such as *Blair Witch Project*, *Ruby In Paradise*, and *George Washington* which contributes to the growing regional awareness and support for independent production. There's also the increasing number of film festivals where films can gain public exposure as well as to companies seeking ready-made films distribution. And of course, there's the advent of various digital formats which bring with them dramatically lower production costs and the potential for a host of alternative distribution venues. Whether independent film will truly able to gain a foothold as an industry here in the Southeast is yet to be seen. As Afemo Omilami puts it, "The only way things are going to change is if we start supporting and developing the young independent writers and directors." See "Independent and Student Films" in the chapter "Getting Exposure" for information on how independents are cast.

Commercials

A commercial is produced by a client in order to sell a product or service. A union-scale regional or national commercial is potentially some of the most lucrative work available to an actor. The commercial market in the Southeast is usually very strong when the economy is strong, but can be unpredictable during other times. So even after you've landed a commercial or two, don't, as they say, quit your day job.

A popular myth about commercials is that you have to be particularly attractive to be successful as a commercial actor. If you pay close attention to commercials you will soon realize this is not the case. Most of the actors you see doing commercials have a look that Mainstream America can identify with — a parent, a teacher, a farmer, a banker, or a customer. If you can look in the mirror and see yourself as representative of any of these or other "types," then you may very well have a good commercial "look." The next step is to find out if the camera will pick it up.

One of the main requirements for commercial actors is that they be completely comfortable in front of the camera. "When a director says jump," says Atlanta-based actor Tommy Housworth, "the response shouldn't be 'How high?' but 'Which way?'" The only way to achieve this kind of agility as an actor is through experience. And the best way to acquire that valuable experience risk-free is by investing the time and energy in the appropriate acting classes. (For more on this, refer to the Training chapter.)

Non-Broadcast

Corporate, Industrial and Educational Film & Video

The category of non-broadcast (sometimes called corporate television or industrial) includes films and videos produced by a business or educational organizations for internal or non-commercial use. These are often used for promotion, training and orientation, or for instruction of some sort. They often involve an on-camera spokesperson (the actor hired as to represent a product or service) coupled with reenactments of business or sales transactions, and occasionally can be very creative in their scripting. Recently however, this category has expanded to include storecasting (we've all seen the closed-circuit mall or supermarket television), phonecasting (the incessant aren't-we-great-can't-we-sell-you-something-else advertising you hear while you're on hold) and Internet voice and video usage.

Industrial copy has a tendency to be technical in nature and can be difficult to memorize, so it's not unusual for an actor to be required to use either a TelePrompTer or an ear-prompter. A TelePrompTer is a video screen which displays the copy as it is being read and spoken by the actor. An ear-prompter is a tape recorder/player into which the actor has prerecorded the copy. The actor then repeats it as it is being transmitted to an audio receiver placed in his ear. As you might imagine, both of these devices require some expertise to use them effectively, but experience with either or both can be a real asset when seeking corporate work. (One word of caution: never misrepresent your level of proficiency with either of these devices. A local actor tells us of being called to replace not one, but two others who said they were skilled in the use of an ear-prompter when they were not. Needless to say those two actors cost themselves a lot more than that one job.)

Although perhaps not artistically rewarding, non-broadcast projects can provide an actor with a steady source of work among otherwise unpredictable markets. Producers frequently use the same actors for many of their projects if the actor is dependable, congenial, available, and can bring that little extra something to the sometimes dry and unimaginative copy. (See the directory for classes that focus exclusively on training for corporate work.)

The Lowdown

Generally speaking,

- There are always more roles for men than for women

- There are always more women actors than men for the available roles

- The most saturated category in any agency is almost always white females from 20 to 40 years of age
- Being bi- or multi-lingual always increases your marketability (but you must have a expert command of the language)
- The opportunities are increasing for ethnic types in particular, partially because the talent pool is smaller, and partially because because in commercial production advertisers often strive to represent a cross-section of the population. "For example,' says Tammy Green of the Green Agency, "as Miami is a huge Spanish-speaking market, we are always on the look-out for fresh Hispanic talent including children, and teens through grandparents."

On the Road Again

If you don't mind the drive (or even the occasional plane fare), there is work to be had throughout the region. A Los Angeles-based director was astounded when he held a casting at the Fincannon & Associates in Wilmington, NC. "I couldn't believe it," he recounts. "The actors came from everywhere! Atlanta, Tampa, Miami, Little Rock . . . it was amazing!" There may be actors who don't make the round trip to other cities for auditions, but we haven't met more than a handful. "If you want to support yourself in this market," adds actor Carl McIntyre,

"you'd better be ready to drive. It's four hours to Atlanta and four hours back anywhere from several times a month to several times a week. And that's just for auditions."

If you can commit to the travel, you may consider listing with an agent within each specific market or state. If you do list with an out-of-town agent, make sure you are available when he calls. If you decline more auditions than you attend, you will see the number of calls drop, and it will be difficult to re-establish the actor/agent relationship at a later date. Give this serious consideration before you start seeking out-of-state representation. That six- to eight-hour round-trip from Wilmington to Atlanta or Atlanta to Orlando gets much longer when there's no booking as a result.

When working out-of-town, keep accurate records of your expenses for your taxes. Deductible expenses include travel, meals, lodging, postage, telephone and other expenses you incur while working, auditioning or interviewing out-of-town.

A note about taxes: the tax laws for the entertainment industry are sometimes complex and always changing. If you keep good records it can pay off in the long run. As you log expenses, you may find it helpful to consult a tax lawyer or service versed in the deductions allowed for independent contractors (those of us who are basically self-employed) and/or those allowed specifically for the entertainment fields.

(For a comprehensive discussion of tax considerations for actors, read **The New Tax Guide for Performers, Writers, Directors, Designers and Other Show Biz Folk** by R. Brendan Hanlon.)

The Product: You

Being an actor, even an unemployed one, is a full time job. Serious pursuit of your career involves developing your talents, looking for work, being able to perform on demand, and packaging yourself correctly. Get a headshot that looks like you, have a pager and voice-mail and always be working on being a better actor.

JUANELL WALKER
TALENT TREK AGENCY

Training

Here's a test. Name a job or career in which you can be hired with absolutely no experience, understanding or investment of time in what is involved in actually doing the job. Pro golfer? Nope. Web designer? Ummm, no. Physician, attorney, accountant? Certainly not. Guitar player? Don't think so… Waiter? Maybe.

So why would you think that a career as an actor would be any different? "You'd never wake up one day and say, 'I think I'd like to go perform a little hip-replacement surgery today,'" muses Steve Coulter. "But because there are no licenses, degrees, or booster shots required, people make that decision all the time in regards to pursuing an acting career." Any newcomer looking to give himself an edge will strive to be fully trained both in the business and in the craft before attempting to enter the professional marketplace. The best actors also realize that training never ends. "The actors we rely on the most are those that never stop studying," affirms agency owner Rebecca Shrager. "They're always exploring, improving and expanding their skills."

But if television commercials are supposed to represent mainstream America, then why do you need training to act in them? Among other reasons:

- So you'll know what the casting director means when she says, "Slate, please."
- So you'll know where to look when you slate, and when you read.
- So you'll know where to hold the copy so more than just the top of your head and your eyelids get on tape.
- So you'll have something to put on your resume.
- So you'll know not to wear white.
- So you'll know not to wear black.

If you want a body of work, and you want to continue to work, you gotta get some kind of substance behind it.

ACTOR BILL NUNN

Learn to act and call me back.

JEN KELLEY, AGENT
PEOPLE STORE

- So you'll get to audition more than once because you didn't make a complete idiot of yourself your first time out.

- So you'll survive the casting tape. If it's obvious you don't know what you're doing, many casting directors will simply rewind the tape and the director or producer will never even see your audition. Believe us, they're doing you a favor.

- So you'll have a chance at getting the job when you're competing against trained professionals who have been doing this for years.

We could go on. Good training will provide solid instruction, valuable camera time, and immediate feedback. You will learn where you fit as a commercial "type". You will learn how to identify your positive qualities, and minimize your negative ones so that they are no longer a factor. You'll gain the confidence that comes from knowing what to expect going into the audition, instead of feeling like you're walking into a black hole. Classes also provide an environment in which to experiment — without the risk of losing the job if the experiment fails.

Improvisational skills are a tremendous asset to any actor, and to the commercial actor in particular. Approximately half of the commercial auditions you will attend have no lines, only a description of the action (if that). Anything you can do for yourself to enable you to think freely when under pressure will be of great benefit to you. Says actor Kathy Payne, "Improv classes keep you on the edge. You learn to think fast — and to follow as well as lead. So, producers and directors watching your audition more likely to stay involved." And when they're

Acting is the only profession I know of where even as a novice you are judged completely and immediately on only a sample of your work.

ACTOR ROBIN O'DELL

---

involved, you'll be remembered. Orlando casting director Kimberly Mullen affirms it from the other side of the camera. "The actor who's mastered improvisation skills is always going to rise above."

If film and television is your goal, you simply have no choice but to be the best actor you can be. Although day player roles may not carry the project, and you may rarely get an opportunity to utilize all your skills, there are already lots of people with whom you'll be competing who have to do this because they can't be content doing anything else. They are trained, they love it, and they're doing everything in their power to make sure they stay ready for any opportunity that presents itself. If we wanted to compete against them, we'd learn to act.

What about **typecasting**? "A look alone will get you one job, maybe," says agent Linda Newcomb of JTA in Charlotte. If you have a specific look and can deliver a line honestly, you may be able to get by without having to act. You may audition for every redneck cop role that comes along, just because you look and sound like a redneck cop. But keep in mind that for every redneck cop "type" who is not an actor, there are plenty of career actors who can play redneck cops as well as haggard CEO's, seasoned reporters and impatient bank tellers. It's quite simple: being a versatile actor increases your opportunities for work.

It takes an incredible amount of work to become a competent, well-rounded actor — if it's something you love, you'll want to be a good as you can be. When you're not working, you should be working out. This is where you'll develop your skills as a beginner and keep them honed as a professional. In this market auditions and jobs can be weeks apart — nobody will want to hear you play a solo if you don't even bother to keep your instrument in tune.

Training Formats

Professional training comes in many packages. We generally recommend working professionals and theatre companies that offer a variety of on-going classes which can provide you with a valuable foundation as well as a haven for exploring and expanding your craft. Types of classes available will include a

---

Find a good acting instructor, no matter what level you're on, and allow yourself to explore choices beyond your natural instincts so as not to be limited by our basic narrow points of view.

AFEMO OMILAMI, ACTOR
INSTRUCTOR, THE OMILAMI ACTING WORKSHOPS

variety short-term or on-going training, from audition to improvisation to scene study. In the beginning, concentrate on taking orientation classes that can help you get a better idea about the work and the business, so you can decide whether this is for you. If you continue, concentrate on classes that focus on developing fundamental acting and audition techniques — the most important things you'll need to compete. Compare instructors and their approaches (not their hype) and see which have the strongest appeal for you and the type of work you seek. After a while you'll begin to develop your own process — or as Orlando agent Sandi Bell puts it, you'll "make your own toolbox."

Of course, there's the theatre itself. Many newcomers don't realize that almost without exception, the most successful (i.e., working) actors have a background that originates in the theatre. "Acting in plays — some of the best classes I've ever taken," affirms actor Rodney Pickel. "Once I began working in theatre I began to understand much more about what I needed to do for on-camera auditions." Remember that theatre is one of the oldest forms of storytelling. It is a screen*play* that we film.

Weekend seminars, frequently offered by casting directors, directors, and professionals from larger markets are usually more expensive but can provide an intensive workout. It can be good supplemental training for concentrating on specific skills such as **cold reading**, for example — or bringing life to a script that you've never seen before. (We equate cold-reading ability to a strong serve in tennis — without it you simply can't compete.)

But before you write your check, get a variety of opinions from previous participants. Ask about the amount of on-camera time and the maximum enrollment allowed (12 to 16 is good for a regular class — if there are more than 20 you could get lost in the crowd). Don't ever feel that your being seen by a director or casting director will depend on whether or not you take every class they offer. Exposure is never a bad thing, but again you should be paying for the material presented, not the opportunity to "be seen." (SAG agents — those franchised by the Screen Actors Guild — are not permitted to profit from any classes they offer. Evaluate non-union agents with schools attached very carefully. "If they offer classes they're a school, not an agency," says Kathy Hardegree of Atlanta Models & Talent.)

After acquiring some degree of experience, many actors form their own study groups that meet on a regular basis. This format allows you to share information, practice being on-camera, and get unbiased feedback from the camera and your peers.

It is important to explore many opportunities for credible acting instruction to find the ones that are right for you. Review the training that's offered in your area. Check the directory listings and agents' waiting rooms. Select those that appeal to you, contact the instructors for additional information, and audit classes for content and compatibility. Credentials are always good, but it's more difficult to learn from an instructor with whom you don't connect. Learn to trust your intuition — not everyone benefits from the same type of instruction.

Just remember, it's your craft; it's your career.

Working as an Extra

If you have never been on the set of a film or television series, and your resume could use additional credits, working as an **extra** (someone who does not have a scripted line) can provide you with some valuable experience. It pays very little — about $40 a day for up to twelve hours — and you'll do a lot of waiting around. But if you are a beginner and can afford to do a day or two of extra work, it is a good way to get a better idea of what is involved in the filmmaking process. Anyone interested in a film career should do it at least once.

To find out about extras casting, call the 24-hour information line for the film office nearest you. (See the directory under Organizations: Film-Related). These "hotlines" list projects in progress, along with the name of the casting director who should be contacted for extra work. Send your headshot and resume to the address provided. You will be contacted if they can use you.

There is also extra work available in commercials. An extra in a commercial is anyone who is not identifiable. It pays better ($100 or more a day), can provide the same experience to beginners, and can give you a chance to be seen by local commercial directors who may recognize you later at a commercial audition. You may also be upgraded to a featured extra and consequently have something for your reel.

We have one word of caution about being an extra. Unless you want to stay an extra (and there are many who are perfectly happy doing just that), don't do any more extra work than can be of benefit to you experience-wise. There is a strong tendency in this industry to pigeonhole people, and if you get known as an extra, it may be difficult to convince anyone that you can do anything else.

Working as a Stand-in

When shooting a film, the most tedious and time consuming work is the "set-up" of each shot. It takes an extraordinary amount of time to get the set and principal actors lit correctly, rehearse the action and coordinate camera moves. So instead of wilting the highly-paid principal actors under hot lights, they hire doubles to suffer for them. For someone with no experience, it's one of the best ways to learn how a film set functions. "You can make friends, ask questions, and put your face in front of a camera all day long," says actor and indie filmmaker Lisa France.

Stand-ins are usually hired though talent agencies. If you're interested, just let your agent know you'd be willing to be a stand-in in whenever they're called.

Or you could do what Danny Vinson did when he heard about a film that was shooting locally. "I called the film commission and got the name of just one person working in the production office. I knew the auditions were on Saturday, so I went over the night before. When I spotted a group of people setting up chairs, I asked them for the person whose name I'd been given." She asked him immediately if he were there to help out, and as a result he became the stand-in for four principal actors for forty-eight shoot days. "And because I was on time and kept my mouth shut," he adds, he was offered work on subsequent films as well over the next several years. "I wouldn't trade anything for those early days," he says. "It was like a university every day." Nine features and sixty-plus commercials later, it seems his "university" training has paid off.

Don't neglect your training in whatever form you choose. It will provide a foundation for continual growth and give you confidence when you're in that never-ending process of selling yourself and your capabilities to others.

Your Speaking Voice

or, "Ah doan ha-yev inny ay-eck see-yunt"

If you have a southern accent, or an accent of any kind, it's best to be able to lose it at will. While it's true that many roles cast throughout the region are southern, or require a specific ethnic, national or regional origin, many more commercial, non-broadcast and film roles will request no accent . You don't have to get rid of it to work, but you'll work more if you can get rid of it when you need to.

As an actor, everyone must be able to understand what you say. Forgive us if that sounds too fundamental, but it is surprising how many beginners tend to overlook this fact. Listen to the way you talk. Do you mumble or chew your words? Do you keep your teeth closed when you speak? Does your speech have a rhythmic or predictable cadence? Can we hear you at all? Dialects, regionalisms, cultural and other personal speech patterns are all mannerisms which can limit your ability to communicate clearly to a majority of the population…and as such will limit your marketability as an actor.

That being said, when roles do call for a specific accent, the truth is no one does it better than someone who has grown up speaking that way. This applies to regional, ethnic or accents of other national origin. In trying to develop an accent that is not your native speech, make sure you are highly proficient before you put it on your resume or demo tape.

For help in this area, check with any of the voice instructors listed in the directory. They offer individual and class instruction, and can assist you in acquiring Standard Mid-American Speech, making improvements in clarity or minimizing distractions in your speech patterns as you begin your career.

The Headshot

As an actor, your key marketing tool is your headshot. It is your business card. It will introduce you to potential employers and representatives who know nothing about you. And for those who do know you, it will remind them of what an engaging, lovable and talented person you really are.

A good headshot should make someone want to meet you, want to know more about you. In a seminar, a former casting director gave her test for a good headshot: have a friend show it to people who don't know you and ask them the question, "Would you let this person buy you a cup of coffee?" Too many negative responses means your headshot is probably not working for you as it should.

There are three types of headshots: commercial, industrial and theatrical. The commercial headshot is the most versatile and is the one we recommend you start out with. Your headshot should look like you — or, like you look when you're having a really wonderful day. The focus should be you — not your jewelry, not your clothing, not the background. Look directly into the lens. Your expression should be open and friendly, and your eyes should communicate something about your personality (which hopefully ranges somewhere between pleasant and scintillating). Get rid of any glamour, attitude and head angles adapted from a JC Penney catalog or GQ magazine. Your significant other may adore it but it won't get you work. "It just makes you look like silly green talent," comments one casting director.

Keep photographic touch-ups to a minimum. If the lines or freckles or bags will be there when the camera rolls, they better be on your headshot as well. When casting directors call for someone in their mid-forties, they don't mean someone in their mid-forties who looks like they're in their mid-thirties with the right makeup and just the right light. Leave the lines alone. You've earned them.

*When we polled professionals about the qualities of a good headshot, the most consistent, immediate and emphatic response was, **Make sure your headshot looks like you!** It infuriates everyone from casting to director to producer when they call in someone based on how they look in the headshot and an entirely different person walks in the door. Says casting director Regina Moore, "If you change, your headshots MUST change!"*

The hair and wardrobe for an industrial headshot incorporates more of a business look, but the expression is still usually relaxed and friendly. The theatrical headshot (used for film and television as well) leans a bit toward the dramatic in both expression and wardrobe. After you're working and you have lots of extra money, you may want additional headshots to target the industrial and film/theatrical market. In our market however, never feel like you have to start out with anything other than a good commercial headshot. We know many actors working in all three areas whose one headshot serves them very well.

Selecting the Photographer

It is very important that you make sure that the photographer you select is a professional headshot photographer. These photographers are in contact with agents and casting people and know what the current requirements (lighting, wardrobe, makeup, etc.) and trends (indoor, outdoor, framing, borders) are in headshot photography in the Southeast. Every market has its own standards (even though they all change from time to time) and it's important when you are starting out that you are able to rely on the photographer for this kind of information. It is only too obvious to an agent or casting director when a shot is produced by a friend, or a commercial or fashion photographer, and it will label you as being even more of an amateur than you are.

We polled area agents and compiled a list of their recommended headshot photographers in the directory. You can find other headshot photographers through word of mouth, or by checking agents' waiting rooms for flyers and business cards advertising headshot photography. Just make sure the photographer you choose is familiar to and recommended by a variety of agencies.

Before making an appointment for your shoot, it is a good idea to schedule an interview with two or three photographers. This will give you a chance to discuss their rates, review their approach, and see examples of their work. In particular, be sure to include in your discussion the conditions under which the photographer will reshoot your session at no additional charge — i.e., what level of dissatisfaction is required, and whose (yours, your agent's, the photographer's). The personal interview serves another purpose in that it allows you to evaluate the chemistry between you and the photographer. It will be important that you are relaxed and able to ask questions as you feel the need — both before and during your session. If you are intimidated by a photographer for any reason, you won't feel comfortable during your session and your headshot will suffer for it.

The Photo Session

Before you begin the shoot, your photographer should know who your agent is and what type of work you will be focusing on. This information along with your interview will help the photographer get a better feel for how you should be photographed and what you should bring to the session in terms of your wardrobe. If you are currently taking any classes, your instructor will also be able to give you assistance in choosing your wardrobe. Make sure you are happy with your hair style before you schedule your photo session. A drastic change in hair style once your headshot is done renders the headshot virtually useless.

Women will require a professional makeup artist who is also familiar with current makeup and hair requirements for headshots. Once you've selected your headshot photographer, ask him to suggest a make-up artist whom he knows and trusts. You will probably do your own hair — only you know what it looks like the majority of the time. It will be the makeup artist's responsibility, however, to check your hair and makeup during the session to make sure everything is as it should be for each shot. Most make-up artists are professionals and will do just that. If you notice that yours seems not to be paying attention, ask a specific question or two as a reminder of where their focus should be.

The best way to make sure you take a great picture is to have fun. The easiest way to do that is to be relaxed. So make sure you do whatever you need to do to relax before and during the session. Meditate. Bring a tape of your favorite music. Put the people, places and situations that delight you right in the lens, and when you're done, you'll have a picture of your personality as well as your face.

Selecting the Print

After your session, the photographer will send you a **contact sheet** for each role of film taken. A contact sheet is used for proofing the shots prior to enlarging them as prints. It displays the entire roll of developed film on an 8"x10" sheet of photographic paper (each print is the size of the negative). Photographers will usually designate their favorites with highlighted dots. Inspect the shots yourself and select your favorites. To see them well enough to judge them properly, you'll need a **loupe** (a small eyeglass used for magnification), which may be purchased at any photography store. Check the quality of each shot. They should be clean and sharply focused with good contrast and no "hot spots" (where lighting that's too strong washes out definition). Sometimes you will see small white spots on the contact prints. These are water spots and will not appear on the print. (If the quality of the majority of the shots is not satisfactory however, ask the photographer for a reshoot.) Let as many experienced people in the business as possible mark their favorite shots. If you are currently taking any classes, your instructor can help you. If you have an agent, let her make the selection. If you don't have an agent, the one or two shots with the most dots wins. Call the photographer and request 8"x10" prints from your final selections.

Reproducing the Print

Now that you have this great print of your perfect headshot, all you need are copies for the teeming multitudes. We have listed several companies that do both photographic and lithographic reproduction. Photographic reproduction involves getting a negative from your print and using that negative to produce prints on photographic paper. It's a fairly expensive process but the quality is very high. Lithographic reproduction is the same process that is used to put a picture in the newspaper. This process costs much less in comparison, but is very good quality and is widely accepted in this market. Which method you choose depends on your personal preference, the local market preference and your budget. Review your choice with your agent or your training professional before proceeding.

We have listed companies that provide both types of service in the directory. All the companies listed have consistent, quality service. To get current rates and other order information, call several companies and have them send you their order forms and/or samples. (There are several photographers who will provide order forms with your print.)

Before you have your print reproduced, look at as many headshots as you can. See what appeals to you in the way of layout, typestyle and name placement. Get other professionals' opinions on various layout options. We prefer the lower right for name placement, so it's at the outside corner when placed in a three-ring binder. Choose a simple, readable typestyle — we are not looking for soul expression here. Then ship or deliver the print along with the order form to the company you've chosen. When you receive your copies, you'll be ready for the next step: attaching your resume.

First impressions stay with us all. A headshot should be a true impression of who you are not only as an actor but also as an individual. An actor should reflect more than a "Hire me" image to the photographers camera lens: this is an opportunity to captivate the still camera with what can offer the moving camera. Make it count — your first impression could be your last.

REGINA MOORE, MOORE-HIGGS CASTING

Your Resume

An actor's resume should contain the following information:

- Name
- Contact information
- Statistics (eye color, hair color, height, weight, sizes, vocal range, etc.)
- Credits
- Training
- Special skills

It should be in a standard format (see example in the Appendix) that is professional, unpretentious and easy to read. We have seen resumes that could win design awards, but we always wonder whether they might be compensating for a lack of something. There is also no need to identify your resume with the word "resume" at the top. We know what it is.

Your Name

Put it in the center at the top and make it big. We want that image (along with your face) burned into the reader's memory. We don't think it's necessary, however, to qualify yourself in any way (Jack Edwards, actor; or Jack Edwards actor/singer). It's redundant. You wouldn't be auditioning if you weren't one, and if you're not, what good is a label?

As important as a good headshot is, it's not everything. Director Bob Newcomb expressed a common opinion about headshots and resumes: "I use them for recall and reference, but actually I'm far more interested in the person and the audition."

Contact Information

Under your name, list a phone number, including area code, where you can be reached. If you have an agent, they will want you to list their business phone. They may want you to use their pre-printed stickers.

If you do not have an agent yet, it is preferable to use a pager or service number and not your home phone. (For more information, see the section on Staying in Touch.) If you do use your home phone, list the number on your resume as "Contact: 000.000.0000" and make sure you have an answering machine or voice mail that states that you can be reached there.

Statistics

These include your height, weight, and the color of your hair and eyes, none of which is discernible from your headshot. Many actors include sizes as well (for men: shirt, slacks, coat and shoe; for women: blouse, skirt, slacks, shoe) as a courtesy for wardrobe. Do not put your measurements on your resume no matter how impressive. If this is a legitimate job, sizes will be sufficient. Another statistic to omit is your age. In this business, you don't really have an age, you have a range, and that is determined by how you look. So in this instance, your age is immaterial.

Credits

Credits should be listed by category: Film, Television, Commercials, Industrials, Theatre. Combine film and television (Film/Television, Film/Non-Broadcast) until you have enough credits to make them separate categories. We've heard lots of opinions on order, but our preference is to list credits according to how you would like to be identified. If you'd like to be known primarily as a commercial actor, list commercials first on your resume. Likewise with film or corporate television. Naturally, if you don't have any credits in these categories yet, you can't put them on your resume. But when you do, keep that in mind.

After you've been working for awhile, many actors create a separate commercial resume and video reel, and under the Commercial category simply state "List of commercials and video reel available on request." Separate resumes can be cumbersome (and costly) to maintain, and somewhat irritating to agents who have to keep up with them. In the beginning one clear, concise resume that is truly representative of the bulk of your work is sufficient and less confusing all around.

We could write an entire book on the different theories of how your credits should be listed — especially when you get into politics and conflicts within the commercial industry — but we won't. We will refer you to our sample in the Appendix for starters, and again recommend that you get to a good class for detailed information from a qualified instructor with whom you can have one-to-one interaction to get all your questions answered. When you get an agent, they'll tell you how they'd like them formatted.

If you don't have specific acting credits yet, list anything that is performance- or entertainment-related, just so that people can get some idea of what you might be able to do. Listing musical performances of any kind, professionally speaking, anytime people were watching you (whether or not you were paid) can help an agent or producer assess your potential as a talent.

Do not include print or modeling credits on an acting resume if you want to be considered an actor. It is a standard perception throughout the industry that models cannot act. Whether or not it is the truth is irrelevant.

The specific information included for each credit can also vary from one individual's resume to another. Some actors include directors they have worked with on film, commercial and/or corporate projects. They say it encourages more relaxed conversation during the audition if people recognize the name. There are also actors who don't necessarily include the theatre or company where they performed if it does not have immediate name recognition — instead they just list the play and the role they played. As you get more experience you'll begin to fine tune your own preferences for credit listings. As long as they're listed clearly and concisely, you can't really make any big mistakes.

Study and Training

Place any university, professional or film school study here. If your instructor has some notoriety, list the individual as well. "To me, training is almost more important than experience," says agency owner Sandi Bell. "It tells me that you take yourself and your work seriously." If you're a true novice, another reason to begin classes right away is that training might be the only thing on your resume. It shows that you are attempting to compensate for the lack of practical experience with educational experience.

Skills

The skills section serves a dual purpose. First of all, there are lots of special skills, interests or activities that could potentially be a requirement for a specific role, such as playing tennis or the expert ability to use an English accent (and we do mean *expert*). If you have any special or unusual skills at which you are proficient, list them in this section. Another purpose this serves is to give the reader a better idea of you as a person — the more they say about you as a non-actor, the more interesting you will be to the reader. As actor Wilbur Fitzgerald puts it, "Have another life and put it on your resume."

One final note on completing your resume: never lie. There's a great deal of interaction within the production community throughout the region, and the last thing you want to be known for is padding your resume. One casting director tells the story of scanning an actor's resume during an audition, only to find to her surprise a credit for a film she herself had cast. To her amazement, the actor even went on to describe his experience on the set.

There's no need to apologize for a lack of experience. Save your imagination for when it will do you the most good — in front of the camera.

Printing Your Resume

Creating a resume on a computer is the easiest way to keep it current. Even if you don't have a computer, there are computer service bureaus and full service printers that will rent you one by the hour. You create your resume yourself and keep it on your own disk, then rent the computer as required keep it updated. There are also services that will maintain your resume for you. You simply supply them with updates and request copies as you need them.

It's important to keep your resume as current as possible, although if you have done work since your last update and you have an audition, go ahead and write in your last credit. We know actors who always have at least one credit written in — they feel it looks like they're working too much to keep their resume updated. Prior to the computer age that may have been the case — we're afraid it looks like you just don't have time to do a good job. Have an updated resume whenever possible — it just looks more professional.

There are many theories on attaching your resume to your headshot. If you have an agent, ask them how they prefer it. We like having the resume printed on the back of the headshot. It takes up less space in the agent's file, the resume can't get separated from the headshot, and it simplifies the update process. Depending on the type of printer you have may be able to print from your own computer, or you can use a service bureau. If you prefer, you can hand-feed lithographed headshots into copiers at many printers for pennies a copy. The quality may be somewhat less than having them printed, but if cost is a major consideration, this method is acceptable. (If you are updating your resume often, be careful not to copy too many or you'll waste a perfectly good headshot once the resume on its back has become obsolete.)

If your agent prefers that you attach your resumes, first have them trimmed to the size of the headshot. You may then glue them — rubber cement and glue sticks are both fine for this purpose, available at any office supply store — or staple them to the back of the headshot. Arguments against these methods are that glue can dry out and your resume can separate from your headshot (which casting people HATE), and staples catch on things and can't be faxed. Both these methods cause a stack of headshots to be fairly bulky in an agent's file, but allow you to update your resume on an existing headshot. Other alternatives include double-stick tape and spray-mount adhesives. Both look good, but are more expensive and are tricky to apply.

Keeping In Touch

It's very important that once you make yourself available for work, you can be reached as quickly, easily and in as few phone calls as possible. Agents, and everyone else in this business, are busy people. They do not have time to try you repeatedly because you haven't returned their calls. And with the speed at which auditions sessions arrive and need to be confirmed, it's imperative that you retrieve messages and return calls as quickly as you can (inside of an hour is a good norm). The fewer phone calls it takes to reach you, the easier it is on your agent, the better they will think of you and the more opportunities you'll be likely to get.

The minimum requirement is an answering machine or service, preferably one that is yours alone. List it on your resume as "Contact" or "Service" only if you do not have an agent. If you are fairly mobile and/or you are beginning to get auditions on a regular basis, consider getting a cell phone (please, keep the battery charged). There are a number of affordable plans available and web sites that allow you to compare them before you buy. Digital pagers also can be leased inexpensively on a month to month basis. A third service is voicemail (which is also an option with cell phones and pagers). Voice mail allows you to keep your home telephone number off your resume, yet affords callers the convenience of leaving a message whether or not they need a return call.

And while we're at it, let's talk about messages. Keeping in mind that whoever is calling you is doing so frequently, and even if your thirty-second Clint Eastwood imitation was funny the first time, it's not now. Take a look at the examples on the next page.

BAD Messages

- Any message that pretends a live person is answering, e.g. "Hello?... hello?... Hah, gotcha! We're not home...."

- Comedy routines. They're not.

- Messages that don't tell us who we've called.

- Long messages that don't tell us how to interrupt them (we don't want to send a fax or call somebody else at another number; we just want to leave a message. Now.)

- Long messages by your children.

- Long recorded songs (the sound quality alone should dissuade you).

- Long recorded live songs.

- Long recorded live songs sung by a child.

- Long, overly religious messages.

- Babies gurgling, or something like "say hi sweetie...say hi, say hi..." followed by a variety of unintelligible sounds for a seemingly endless amount of time. People really do this.

GOOD Messages

- Short messages.
  Any short message is good.

Adapted from **The Actor's Guide for Kids**
by Jen Kelley & Brenda Krochmal

Wardrobe

It is not uncommon on both union and non-union shoots to be asked to supply all or part of your own wardrobe (on a union shoot you will be compensated for it, otherwise you will not). If you can do so quickly and effortlessly, it's another way to be identified as a professional, which can only help you in the future. So it's to your benefit to have wardrobe on hand to suit any of the following types you think you may be auditioning for, and working as:

- upscale casual
- upscale dress
- blue-collar man/woman
- dad/mom (grandfather/mother)
- business or corporate man/woman
- sportsman/woman (fishing, tennis, aerobics, etc.)

The dress appropriate for the different types varies a great deal. Watch current commercials to check current styles, and use your on-camera classes to test various wardrobe choices. When building your wardrobe, it helps to choose colors that look good on you, and on camera. White and pastels are not good because they are highly reflective and will ruin the lighting on your face. Too much black is not good because it can look formless and non-dimensional on camera. Rich colors usually work well, but the best test is to see it on camera yourself.

Another tip: some incredibly organized actors we know keep several wardrobe alternatives in the car with them. It is unfortunately not unusual to go to an audition for a young mother and find out when you get there that the role is actually a young mother at her job as an office manager. A jacket or dress hanging in the back seat "just in case" enables you to make a painless transformation. It can take time to build a camera-ready wardrobe, but it will pay off over the long run if you plan to continue in the business.

When your wardrobe is supplied for you, you may be asked to come in for a fitting. If you are, you will be compensated for your time. Check with your agent for the correct rate.

As you begin to audition, especially for commercials, you'll notice actors appearing for doctor roles in hospital scrubs, postal worker roles with mailbags, etc. "Do I have to find all that?" you ask. We would say no. If you have a few items that might compliment the various roles you commonly audition for, that's fine. But don't worry about stocking your closet with every professional uniform you can think of... you're auditioning for the role, not the wardrobe consultant. "Unless we request something specifically," says casting director Mark Fincannon, "I personally prefer that that actors dress casually and just come prepared to work their talent."

In the Market

*Never transfer the responsibility of your career to anyone else:
not an instructor, not an agent, not a casting director. Trust
those you've chosen to work with, but you make the decisions;
you maintain the control.*

KATHY HARDEGREE
ATLANTA MODELS & TALENT

The Talent Agent

What does an agent do? An agent does not get you work: that's your job. An agent's job is to provide you with an opportunity to get work, and to negotiate your contract whenever possible. An agent's customers are casting directors, producers and directors.

Walk a Mile in My Shoes

The more you know about what goes on inside an agency, the better you'll be able to relate to them. Typical activity at a busy agency goes something like this:

Shirley is the receptionist and talent coordinator at All Types Talent. She is on the phone with two lines holding. "Martha, Kimberly's on four! She's wants to set up a casting tomorrow morning..." She punches line three. "Good afternoon, All Types. Can I help you?"

Nancy G is the owner/agent, on the phone to a casting director. "So you're seeing Warren, Alan, and Andi at 11, 11:10, and 11:20 Tuesday. What about Steve Westen? He's new but he's good. He's done a lot of stage and a couple of regional spots. I really think you should see him for the Dad."

Martha is her partner, also on the phone. "...so Jim is confirmed and his call is at 10. Diane is confirmed and her call is at 11:30. You're faxing directions and contacts? Great. Thanks Sherry." She takes line four. "Hi Kimberly, it's Martha, how are ya?"

Shirley is now making calls trying to set up audition times. After waiting for an actor's Really Cute Message to be over, she leaves her own. "Cynthia, it's Shirley at All Types. We have an audition for you tomorrow at 10 at Anthony's. Please call to confirm."

Now she calls, "Nancy, it's Jack on two. He wants to know if Pride & Melissa are confirmed for the PSA on Friday." Nancy picks up line one by mistake. "Hi Jack. How…"

"Hi there. I'm calling because I was thinking about getting into acting and I was wondering what I should do to get started."

If you were an agent and not an actor, you would understand why they wish you'd asked someone else this question first. "Since the majority of my work is done on the phone," says Jackie Pressley of Capital Artists of North Carolina, "questions like 'Can you tell me what you do there' or demands like 'I'm perfect for the NBC series and you NEED to get me in,' are a real irritant, and assure me that you are not someone in whom I want to invest time and energy." Makes sense, doesn't it? Taking the time to understand a little more about the business and offering the same consideration you'd prefer to receive will go a long way toward making someone not only remember you, but think of you fondly when they do.

Dealing With Agents

As we've seen, agents are busy people. They are not making money when they are on the phone talking to you. Keep the following guidelines in mind when dealing with agents:

- Do send your headshot and resume (attached, please) to the address listed in the directory. (See the Yellow Pages under Boxes for companies which supply 8"x10" cardboard chips to keep your headshot from bending in the mail.)

- Once you've sent it, wait for a reply. Don't drop in or call to schedule an interview. You probably won't get past the receptionist who will simply ask you to submit your headshot and resume. Several weeks after sending your initial mailing, you may do a follow up call to see when you might expect a reply.

- If you know an actor represented by a particular agency (and he knows you and your work), you can ask him if he could drop your headshot off, or if you might use him as a contact.

Agency owner Kathy Hardegree recalls taking a phone call late one afternoon after their receptionist had left. "AMT, this is Kathy." "Hi, I'm someone with no experience and I'd like to be an actor. What should I do?" Kathy took the time to ask some questions, then told the caller she needed to get some training, do some reading, perhaps audition for some theatre and, when the newcomer got a headshot she'd be happy to take a look at her contact sheets. The woman's response was "I don't really want to do all that. Is there someone else I can talk to?"

referral on your submission. Never do this without the actor's permission, however.

- Do be persistent in your mailings. The first time an agency sees you they may have too many of your type to take you on. As you acquire more experience or if conditions change at their agency, they may be more interested at a later date. When informing an agent of other work you've done, it's a matter of courtesy not to mention another agent's name. As Kathy Hardegree reminds you, "Promote, don't brag."

- Don't be rude, ever, unless you don't want to work, ever. This includes receptionists and administrative assistants. You want them to like you — they may offer the first opinion of you the agent hears...and quite frankly offers a great deal more insight into your personality than any interview. In addition, today's receptionist is tomorrow's agent, and many do submissions when the agents are too busy.

- Don't take it personally if you are not signed. They may already have one or more of your type (exclusive or with a preference) which would cause a conflict if they signed you, and not allow them to represent you effectively. Be patient. Try other agencies, or check back with them in three to six months. If you truly have something to offer, you will find your niche.

Some agents have open days when they will see new talent on a walk-in basis. Call specific agencies to verify current

PLEASE don't fax me a headshot...It looks awful and it uses up all my toner. And don't send me one to download. It's takes forever and since don't have the space to store it I have to delete it anyway!

TRACI DANIELLE, OWNER AND SENIOR AGENT
BREVARD TALENT & MODEL AGENCY

information, and to ask what you should expect in the interview. Bring a headshot and resume, or a contact sheet if that's all you have. You'll probably be required to do a short monologue and a cold reading. "I always ask for a cold reading during an interview. It tells me a lot more about an actor's skill level than a monologue," observes Orlando agent Sandi Bell. If the thought of doing either terrifies you, you are not yet ready to approach an agent or go to an audition. Get some training first. Who said, "You only get one chance to make a first impression"?

Once You're Signed

- Keep your headshots and resumes up-to-date and in plentiful supply.

- Do ask what is the best way to keep in touch once you are signed (call-in once a week; send post cards; don't call).

Always ask: different agents are adamant about which they prefer.

- For auditions, keep your requests for special time/day considerations to an absolute minimum. Agents receive specific slots from casting directors and have little flexibility in this area.

- Do look for opportunities for agents to see you in as many varied roles as possible.

- Do **book out**, or let your agent know when you are going to be out of town, and when you will be back. Nothing is more embarrassing for an agent who submitted you to have to tell a casting director that you're not around and she was not aware of it.

- Never call an agent at home.

- Don't call every week after you've worked to see if your payment is in. For non-union jobs, allow at least 60 days (30 for the client to pay the production company, 30 for the production company to pay your agent), then call if you haven't received payment in that time. The agency usually will have contacted the production company by then and can give you an idea of when you can expect payment. Union jobs have a specific payment schedule, so this should not be an issue.

- Do be conscious of your agent's time commitments. When you need to call, be brief and to the point, and always have pen and paper in hand. For example:

Seriously irritating:

Agent: Talent Supreme, this is Isa.

Actor: Hi, this is John.

Agent: John . . .

Actor: John Bolton. How are you?

Agent: (sees two lines blinking on her phone) Fine, John. Can I help you?

Actor: Oh, yeah. I'm returning a page. Man, it's hot isn't it?

Agent: (doesn't know about the weather) A page from…

Actor: Uh…number 4?

Agent: Carol, it's John Bolton returning your page…

Our Dream Actor:

Agent: Talent Supreme, this is Isa.

Actor: Hi, Isa. This is John Bolton returning a page from number 4 to confirm an audition.

Agent: Carol, it's John Bolton returning your page…

ADAPTED FROM **The Actor's Guide for Kids**
BY JEN KELLEY AND BRENDA KROCHMAL

- Don't ask an agent (or a casting director) for his opinion on other agents. If he has one, he's not going to tell you. If you are concerned about a particular agent's reputation, gather the various opinions of professionals you meet in classes and other venues.

It's also important to let your agents know anytime you work, and anytime they can see your work (on television, in the theatre, in a showcase, etc.).The better they know what you can do, the better they can represent you. The best way to do this is via postcards with your headshot on them (you can order these when you have your headshot reproduced) either delivered or mailed. Agents like reminders they can hold in their hands. (Would they prefer e-mail? Ask them!)

For each audition we are only allotted a limited number of slots, so we choose carefully. If we give you a space, it's important that you make a Herculean effort to get there and be on time. If you miss your appointment we don't have time to fill your slot with another person, and that means everyone loses — most particularly you because your talent wasn't showcased. That loss, however innocent, does NOT make an agent happy.

SALLY VAUGHAN, AGENT AND FORMER CASTING DIRECTOR

Multi-listing and Preference

In some parts of the region, many actors (especially newcomers) free-lance. That is, they are signed with more than one agent simply because there is a variety of work (principally non-broadcast and voice-over) available through different agents. For these non-broadcast or regional projects the list of roles and descriptions are provided by the producing staff directly to a specific agency for casting. For larger projects however, Breakdown Services, Ltd. supplies lists and descriptions of roles being cast to all agents and casting companies who subscribe to the service: commercials, feature film and television, etc., so multi-listing in these categories is less of a benefit. However, it is up to the casting director to determine the number slots allotted for individual agencies.

Multi-listing sounds like a great idea, but it can also be very messy. You can't possibly develop as strong a relationship with several agents as you can with one, and turning down one agent's calls repeatedly because you've already been called by another for the same audition does not help. Multi-listing can also softens the market by allowing producers to shop rates, especially for non-union work. "When an actor is multi-listed it kills my negotiating power," adds agent Jimmi McCarter. In addition it's confusing for casting directors trying to remember which agency to contact to request you.

One way to ease some of the confusion and provide your agent additional incentive to submit you is to sign a preference form for a specific casting director. This form specifies that if another agency submits you along with the preferred agency, the preferred agency will get the booking. This practice is most common for commercial casting.

A **preference** form is not a contract; it is a courtesy and should be honored. As an act of faith it is a good way for new or new-to-the-area talent to begin to solidify a relationship with an agent. But before you sign, you should feel confident that this agent will be able to get that particular casting director to see you, because once you declare your preference, any attention you may have received from the non-preferenced agents will evaporate. We know some actors who divide agent preferences equally among various casting directors.

Once you have signed a preference with one agent, it is a professional courtesy to immediately inform any other agents who may be submitting you. It may not be what they want to hear, but better from you than from the casting director after they've wasted their time through several submissions wondering why you are never seen through them. "An actor came in the office the other day and told me they had signed a preference with another agent for a specific category," relates Randall Edwards of Atlanta Models & Talent. "My immediate reply was 'Thank you for letting me know.' That kind of consideration is unfortunately pretty rare."

This is not a race. I am not going to break my neck to call someone first when I know they are with another agency.

JIMMI MCCARTER, OWNER/AGENT
THE CANNON GROUP

Exclusivity

When you sign an **exclusive** contract with an agent, you are saying that only that agency will represent you in a specified category, and with some agencies across the board. Exclusive representation is standard for film and television, and once you're reasonably established you may consider commercials as well. It's rarer for non-broadcast because individual agents have their own clients. Before the contract is offered the agent should, and probably will, have a good idea of what your abilities are so that he can properly represent you. An agent will naturally always submit, always push and negotiate harder for their exclusive people, but keep in mind that other agents will (and should) ignore you in the exclusive area.

When considering exclusive representation, you should be confident not only in your agent's abilities, but how he sees you as a talent, and how he in particular can help your career. There are no hard and fast rules about making the decision to sign exclusive. If you're new to the business, it's usually a good idea to wait until you're confident in what you have to offer, accustomed to the market and have worked with a few agents in order to understand to which agency you are best suited. However, if a particular agency provides you with some great opportunities that pan out for you, consider an exclusive contract to cement the partnership.

Before signing a preference form or an exclusive contract, ask your agent how many individuals are already signed in your category. If there are too many, you may not get submitted as often as some of the talent who has been represented longer. A good agent won't even ask you to sign if they don't think they can give you the proper representation. Just make sure you and your agent have a good understanding of what you can expect before you sign.

Your relationship with your agent is a partnership. Your part is being professional, conscientious, competent, available, and doing your share of the marketing. His is getting you into the auditions for which you are suited, promoting you to potential clients, and negotiating your contract. When both parties do their part, everybody wins. If you feel you are doing your part and still are not getting the auditions, approach your agent for any suggestions he might have. If you still feel you're not getting the representation you deserve, it may be time to look elsewhere for a better fit.

(For some excellent advice on dealing with agents, read **Your Film Acting Career** by M.K. Lewis. It's written for the Los Angeles market but a good deal of what he writes is applicable anywhere.)

OUR DREAM ACTOR . . .

- has professional training, theatre and improv background
- is easy to reach
- returns calls promptly
- keeps address, e-mail and phone information current with the agency
- keeps materials stocked and up-to-date (headshots, resumes, demo tapes)
- looks like their headshot, and has 10 to 15 with them always
- let's us know when they will be out of town and for how long
- confirms audition appointments, and doesn't cancel them at the last minute
- always attends confirmed auditions, and is always on-time (early)

"Don't make more work for me, make less," says former agent Judy Cook.

The Casting Director

Casting directors coordinate the casting process for a commercial, film or telev sion production. Their job is to present the producers and directors that hire them with the best possible candidates for the roles they need to fill. "I'll go anywhere to find the right actor for the role," says casting director Tracy Kilpatrick. "That's why they hire me, and that's why I love my job. I'm there to do the best job for the film, the director, the producer AND the actor."

Casting offices will receive a breakdown of a list and description of roles being cast, either from Breakdown Services or directly from the production coordinator. The casting director then allocates a certain number of time slots to each agency they contact, and the agents submit names and/or headshots of the actors they think are best suited to the available roles. Casting directors will also request to see specific actors with whom they are familiar. "The casting process is essentially solving problems," comments actor Wilbur Fitzgerald.

It's important that casting directors know who you are and what you are capable of doing. This is another part of your agent's job. Some casting directors offer worthwhile seminars and classes in which you can learn more while simultaneously establishing a relationship with the casting director. However, seminars and classes taught by casting directors are not necessarily for the rank beginner. You may benefit more from this type of training if you've had enough prior instruction to be at ease interpreting copy in front of the camera. Never feel however, that the potential for being called for an audition depends on whether or not you take a workshop.

Once your agent knows what you can do, she may be able to convince a casting director to see you. While a lack of experience will sometimes be overlooked if you have a particular look or skill needed at the time, it's very important that you remember that

> *We'll see every actor we need to until we find the one who breathes life into role as it is envisioned by the director and writer.*
>
> LISA MAE FINCANNON
> FINCANNON & ASSOCIATES

anytime you are auditioning for a particular production, you are also on a general audition for the casting director. Even if you are not cast, if you do a good job you will probably be called in to audition again.

Once your are seen by a casting director through a particular agent, it will be through that agent that the casting director expects to locate you. So it only makes sense to consider a preference, if not an exclusive agreement. Says Mark Fincannon of Fincannon and Associates, "The moment I meet an actor, I immediately associate them with the agent that sent them, That way, from then on, I know *exactly* how to find them."

Dealing with Casting Directors

- Don't EVER call a casting director (this includes you too, Mom), even after you've established a personal relationship. Keep in mind it is your agent's job to represent you to the casting director and you may do yourself a lot more harm than good by attempting to make the contact uninvited. You may return calls from a casting director. If there happens to be an announced open call, show up at the appointed time. Other than that, DON'T CALL.

- Don't call casting directors and ask to be seen for a particular role. That's your agent's job. If your agent isn't doing it, look for another agent.

- Do let casting directors know when and where you can be seen, preferably by postcard. Offer complimentary tickets,

but don't pester. Even if the casting director can't attend, there may be someone in the office who can. It will also be apparent that you are out doing what you love, not sitting at home waiting for the phone to ring.

- Do find out who the assistant casting coordinators are and deal with them as professionally as you would the casting director — no matter how they deal with you. (Sometimes life in a casting office can get pretty frantic — take it on the chin, not personally.)

- Don't call the casting director with questions about an audition, such as what to wear, shoot dates, what it pays,

---

Linda Higgs of Moore-Higgs Casting tells of an actor who complained about the receptionist in her office. "I just don't know about that person at the desk," said the actor.

"Really?" replied Linda, "Gosh, I've known her for decades, she usually has much more patience than I. What did she say?"

"She told me I had to wait my turn!" huffed the actor.

"Well, she's just trying to be fair to everyone, I suppose," mused Linda. "my sister's very tolerant with people normally."

A rather severe lesson in grace, wouldn't you say?

etc. Your agent should have been given any available information with the breakdown. If she wasn't, then your agent should call for additional details, not you.

- Don't send unsolicited headshots or demo tapes unless you're sure it's the casting director's policy to accept them.

As an actor, the majority of contact you'll have with a casting director is when you are auditioning. An audition is essentially a job interview, and should be treated as such. Bring at least two headshots, resumes attached, and have more in the car. "Your headshot is your business card," emphsizes casting director Annette Stilwell. As a newcomer, having a professional approach can go a long way toward making up for a lack of experience. "I've had actors interrupt me on the phone with a client to ask for scissors to trim their resume," she adds. So come to the audition prepared. "Find out as much as you can about the job beforehand," advises Annette. "Know the client, the product, the producer, the shoot dates, the callback dates and the copy. It will help you, me *and* your audition."

Patience, Patience

And finally, you must learn patience and flexibility. If you were called to read for the attorney and when you arrive they ask you to read the farmer (or the farmer's wife), don't launch into the standard but-I-worked-on-this-all-night whiney actor tirade. There are a host of circumstances, almost always out of

> *I find the casting process to be almost like a chess game. The good actors will always be in the game until the end. . . it's just that they may be moved from one roll to another as we explore where each best fits in the overall story.*
>
> Mark Fincannon, Fincannon & Associates

the casting director's control, that could cause an apparant lack of organization. Frequently they're working on several projects at once. If it's extremely busy, "It's not unusual that we've had t me to read the script only once or twice before auditions begin," explains Mark Fincannon. Perhaps that role's beer cast, o written out, or altered in some way. Commercial and film scripts are constant state of rewrite, and as an actor you're bound to be caught in the middle sooner or later.

Remember too that when several actors are being considered for a role, the director will sometimes ask for the casting director's opinion on the actors as individuals. After all, they'd most likely know more about them personally. Wouldn't you as a casting director recommend that actor whom you know to take their work seriously and be easy to work with on the set?

So just keep brushing up on your cold-reading skills (did we mention training?), ask for the time you need to prepare, and be one of those actors they remember as exceptionally gracious and understanding.

Getting Exposure

In this business, the more people who know who you are and what you can do, the better. So it will only be to your benefit to avail yourself of any opportunity to promote yourself and what you have to offer (without making a pest of yourself, of course). One way to do that is by staying in contact the people who produce the work.

Contacting producers

Once you become familiar with what work as an actor demands, and are confident in your ability to meet those demands, you may want to find out more about the ad agencies and production companies in your area, who their clients are and what kind of work they generally do. Even if you choose not to introduce yourself by sending them your headshot and a letter of introduction (which takes a great deal of effort on your part and can be expensive), you'll be way ahead by knowing something about the people who are doing the work.

Every state film office will publish a list and/or production guide (often available online) that contains a directory of companies and individuals working in the film and video industry. It may not be a complete listing if only those who've paid the listing fee are included, but it is probably the most comprehensive source of film and video producers, directors and production companies available for each state. These are the people who need to be aware of who you are and what you do. The magazine **Ad Weekly** can give you a good idea of what ad agencies are in town and what accounts they have.

"Go do a play — that's the real deal. After eleven years as a performer and an instructor, it's still the best advice I can give you."

ACTOR BILL NUNN

Never walk out the door without your house keys and your headshots.

LISA FRANCE,
ACTOR/INDIE FILMMAKER

Your letter should be in standard business format. It should simply state your purpose, which is to introduce yourself and inform them of your availability. Include any other pertinent information, such as significant training or familiarity with an ear prompter (which will also be on your resume, if applicable.) Thank them for their time, and inform them that you hope they will consider you when casting projects in the future.

This may not produce direct results, but if nothing else, your face may be familiar when your agent submits your headshot and they may decide to give you a try.

You may also want to consider contacting producers directly, especially in the corporate television market (many of the larger corporations produce their videos in-house). Call the producer, introduce yourself, offer to drop off your headshot and possibly have a brief meeting. This gives you a chance to become a human being instead of just a headshot, which can be a big advantage in this business. Again, it takes a concerted effort to do the required research, but this is how you plan to make your living, right? We know of an actor who estimates that he gets sixty to seventy percent of his corporate work through personal effort. He has a business card file of over 900 contacts and tries to make a minimum of five calls a day.

Your Reel

Anytime you work you should check with the production company on how to get a dub, or copy, of the project, or at least your scene, for your reel. A video reel is a visual resume, consisting of selected samples of an actor's professional work, compiled to give the viewer an idea of versatility in look and talent. It's a good marketing tool once you have enough work, especially for an agent's out-of-town customers. Sometimes commercial and corporate work can be booked from a reel alone.

(Notice we were specific about a reel consisting of professional work. Don't put acting class work on your reel no matter how good you, or anyone else, think it is. Production professionals are highly sensitive to production quality. Sound and lighting conditions are invariably poor in any class and would compromise De Niro at his most powerful — imagine what it could do to you.)

If possible, get the video copy on beta or digital stock — it's more expensive, but the reproductive quality is far, far superior to VHS. To save some money and still get your high-quality dub, buy one empty thirty- or sixty-minute beta tape to use as a stack reel to collect all your work, and then have whoever is making your copies use that whenever possible. As digital formats become more common, it may be DVDs and CDs that you are requesting (and will then have available on your web site). Stay tuned!

Before putting together your own reel, get sample reels from your agent or fellow actors for ideas on format. Businesses who will rent you editing facilities can be found in telephone business directories under "Video Production".

The Play's the Thing

There's nothing like working in the theatre. You'll to acquire solid acting experience and get great exposure in the process. Contact theatres and check audition notices for individual productions, or find out when general auditions are held for the professional theatres in your area. There are also general unified auditions held throughout the year by theatre conferences and other related organizations where you may audition with appropriate monologues or perhaps a song or two for a multitude of theatre companies at once (check the Directory for these organizations). If you are cast in a production, contact your agents and let them know the performance dates. Follow-up with a phone call and if they will commit to a specific date, arrange to have complimentary tickets left at the door (most theatres will have no problem with this). For more information on keeping your agent informed of your work, see the chapter on Agents.

There are also acting instructors who produce showcases (live and/or taped) one or more times per year. These will consist of a variety of short scenes by students where agents, casting directors, directors and other professionals in the industry will be invited to attend. A reputable showcase can be a very good opportunity to meet and be seen by these people. Ask about showcases when you are auditing classes: how often they are produced, what are the requirements for participation, etc. Beware that showcases vary in quality, however, and it could do you more harm than good to appear in one which is sub-standard.

Independent and Student Films

Anywhere there is a film institute or a university with a department of film studies, there is an opportunity to be in short, experimental and student films. The days can be long and the pay non-existent, but it can also be very educational, an opportunity to get a clip for your reel and some of the most fun you can have. Recounts Steve Coulter: "I learned how to act in film by doing student films. One of my fondest memories from living in New York was when I'd hop on a subway after working all night at a bar, take a 45 minute train ride up to the Bronx to shoot an NYU student movie. There was no money, stale doughnuts, and we were freezing to death. But I had the time of my life, because it was a great group of people and we were all doing something we loved."

Independent films run the gamut in type, budget and quality in general (although there's not necessarily a correlation between budget and quality). Higher budget films can afford to cast through normal casting/agent channels, and can be virtually indistinguishable from their Hollywood counterparts. Smaller budget independents may cast through everything from word of mouth, to postings at non-profit film organizations and other film communities, to the standard ad in the arts section of the classifieds. If there is any budget at all, the local film commission should be aware of it and you can call the hotline to find out where you can submit your headshot. As you begin to be more connected to the film community, you will also become familiar with the independent casting channels.

Sometimes due to lack of experienced personnel, smaller budgeted films may be a bit more haphazard in their operation. The shooting schedule may approach that of what we affectionately refer to as "guerrilla filmmaking." There is rarely any pay, and if you opt for deferred payment, understand that it will be virtually the same as gratis. But if it's a good project and your heart is in it, you'll have the time of your life no matter what the demands. So whenever possible, read the entire script, assess the quality of the project and choose your films carefully. "A worthwhile role will never involve anything immoral or illegal," advises agency owner Kathy Hardegree. If you're going to devote time, effort and a good portion of your life, our advice is to make sure someone else has put the same effort into crafting a good story to tell and learning the best way to tell it.

Web Casting

As the Internet has evolved, so has the idea that hey, we don't need agents and casting directors to get ourselves cast, we just need our headshot on a web site. Every day there is yet another web site which offers you the opportunity (for a fee, of course) to catalog your headshot and resume with the idea of bypassing the normal casting channels. Although we are personally of the opinion that having your headshot and resume on your own page could never be a bad idea, we also believe that the odds of being called to read for any project you'd actually be interested in from one those sites is practically nonexistent.

One reason that producers and directors use agents and casting directors is that at any given moment there are hundreds, and potentially thousands of job applicants for every available role. Some of them are professionals, some are not. Some should be seen, some should not even be in the business. (Now be honest, don't you think you are right for EVERYTHING?) If you were a producer or director, would you have the inclination or desire to download pages of miniscule black-and-white photos to decide which resume you might want review, choose someone you don't know and then call to see if they might want to read for a project they know nothing about? This may change as standard bandwidths increase in capacity. But until then, this industry will continue to prefer 8x10s they can hold in their hands, of actors someone knows something about, with eyes they can see into and resumes only a flip away.

You will always hear the "it's who you know" complaint from various unhappy actors. We would reword that to say that it's definitely a people-to-people business. If you were spending $2 million of someone else's money to make a small film on which could depend the rest of your filmmaking career, who would you consider reading? A teeny little black & white person or someone everyone knows is an experienced, versatile actor who's great to work with? (This doesn't mean your agent might not scan your headshot, keep it on file and then submit it electronically as requested. When broadband becomes the norm, we predict this form of submission will become the standard).

Generally (and there are certainly exceptions), independents with a budget will use an agent or a casting director to present them with actors whose work they know, who have adequate experience and who are right for the roles being cast. Lower budget projects may cast through an ad, word-of-mouth, or place notices at various film-associated venues. With experience, you'll learn how to stay apprised of what's going on in the region.

But please remember that your very best marketing tool is the work you do and who you are as a human being. As one casting director says, "Just do good work. It'll be in the network and people will know about it."

Unions

There are two types of productions: those whose contracts are negotiated by a professional union, and those whose are not. The unions for film and television are:

- SAG   The Screen Actors Guild

- AFTRA   American Federation of Television and Radio Artists

As a rule, feature films are always under SAG's jurisdiction, while radio and sound recordings are always covered by AFTRA. Beyond that, all other types of productions are up for grabs, including live and video-taped television shows, soaps, commercials, non-broadcast production, and all things digital. At this writing the entire industry is undergoing a massive sea change while coming to terms with usage considerations that encompass all types of productions in all forms of media now in common use, such as digital features on various interactive and Internet venues, DVDs, CDs, broadband, etc.

A union shoot is operated within the provisions set out by SAG or AFTRA governing pay rates, overtime, compensation for mileage, wardrobe, residuals for re-broadcast, etc. There are set payment schedules. The union can also intervene in cases of non-payment and other disputes concerning union contract provisions.

Non-union productions have no set standard provisions. You are paid according to the rates outlined by the individual production. There are no residuals for re-broadcast of a non-union production (this is termed as a **buy-out**), so the amount that you are paid covers both the actual shoot and the amount of time the spot is allowed to broadcast: in the markets specified, as often as they like. This is called the cap; six-months to one year is common. Keep in mind, however, that there is no organization policing the terms of a

I prefer the most professional talent I can find, and usually that means union.

ROXANNE MCMILLAN
OWNER/AGENT, RTA

non-union contract. If the terms are violated it will be up to you and your agent to obtain the additional payments.

It's your responsibility on any contract (but particularly on non-union contracts) to know exactly who is paying you, what you're getting paid, what it covers before you do the shoot. If you don't get paid on a non-union shoot, it's then up to your agent to intervene for you. (This situation occurs more often than we would like to think. Talk to any actor with a moderate amount of experience and chances are he's been stiffed at least once.) Getting the money you are owed can be a long and painful process, so it always helps to be as informed as possible about the specifics of the job.

Just as there are two types of productions, there are two types of agencies: union-franchised and non-union, depending on the type of work the agency books. The number of franchised agencies varies greatly from state to state in the region. For example, in Florida almost every agency is franchised, but there are almost none in North Carolina and Alabama and South Carolina. Georgia and Tennessee have a mix of franchised and non-union agents.

When considering a non-union agency, do your homework. Through your classes you can learn a lot about the reputations of the various agents so that you may feel more comfortable about who to approach for representation. Although you'll gather diverse comments, opinions will be amazingly consistent for the disreputable ones. It's also not a bad idea to have more than one non-union agent because not every agent has access to every non-union client, but each market has its own standard. Take the time to find out what it is in your area.

The union/non-union issue plays a much bigger part in a right-to-work state. There are twenty-one right to work states throughout the country, as are all of the states in the mid-Atlantic and southern regions (Alabama, Arkansas, Georgia, Florida, Kentucky, Louisiana, Mississippi, North Carolina, South Carolina, Tennessee and Virginia). In New York and Los Angeles, once you are booked on a union shoot, you must join before you can work on another (there is a grace period). However, in a right-to-work state you cannot be prevented from working on a union job because you are not a member of the union. This is of course to your benefit because it allows you to gain valuable experience while assessing for yourself the benefits of union membership.

To join a union in a right-to-work market is always a highly personal decision. If you are dependent on your income as an actor, that alone can be a factor because so much of the work is non-union, and once you join, you are considered a professional and as such are prohibited from doing non-union work.

We are personally of the opinion that the pay scale established by the union indirectly influences non-union compensation as well, because outside of a market with a strong union presence, you will generally be paid less for your work. And to be frank, there is absolutely no other entity on the face of the planet that gives one whit for the rights and interests of actors (we are a dime a dozen, as they say). So once the bulk of the work you do is union and you begin receiving benefits (and both unions offer generous health and pension plans), it only makes sense to us to contribute to the organization that provides them to you.

That said, joining a union doesn't make you better actor, nor will it bring you work. If you're fairly new to the business, joining before you have enough experience to qualify you as a professional just doesn't make sense. Don't assume that by joining you will automatically be eligible for better opportunities. Generally when a director, producer or casting director sees a union affiliation, they assume a certain level of skill and experience, which they expect to see reflected on your resume.

For this reason, many actors outside a major market wait to join the union until they've developed their skills doing both union and non-union work. Beyond that, it's a personal decision depending on your goals, both short- and long-term.

(For a terrific explanation of what unions are and how they work, read **How To Be A Working Actor** by Mari Lyn Henry and Lynne Rogers. Or, contact your local SAG/AFTRA office.)

Union/Non Union Comparison

	SAG/AFTRA	Non-Union
Pay Scale	Established pay scale*	Negotiated
Overtime compensation	Established overtime rates	Rare; negotiated
Residuals for broadcast/theatrical	Yes, buy-outs available	No; term buy-outs common
Payment schedule	Yes (up to 30 days)	No
Wardrobe/Make-up	Usually supplied	Often actor responsibility
Contract	Always	Agent voucher/contract
Taxes, FICA	Withheld	Actor responsibility
Pension & Welfare, Medical	Yes, with est. minimum earnings	No
Mileage/travel/per diem	Established minimums	Negotiable

* Theatrical films are the exceptions. With the advent of independent film and widely-varying budgets, all SAG contracts can be negotiated individually.

Just Flip the Burgers

The Process

"It's faster all the time — too fast. It's as if it all happens in compressed time," says director George Watkins of Synergy Films, acknowledging the impossible demands in the world of commercial production. "They come in fast and furious and we're never ready," concurs agency owner Roxanne McMillan, speaking of winter nationals commercials that like Florida snowbirds arrive in droves from October to March to take advantage of Florida climate and locations. "They want it all and they want it now," she adds.

For a commercial, ad agencies and their clients agonize for months over decisions concerning the message, the format and all the specifics involved in marketing their product or service. "People have bled over the spoken word," emphasizes actor/writer/instructor Shannon Eubanks. But by the time the casting process is taking place, the ball is rolling at a horrendous pace: the client is making last minute changes and the script is still being revised. The director is finalizing location arrangements, confirming pre-production schedules with the shooting crews and negotiating post-production requirements, sometimes in phone calls between one audition and the next.

Casting is only one cog in this highly convoluted process. The more you understand this, the more you'll be appreciated for your flexibility, and the less likely you'll take any resulting actions personally. (See the Appendix for representative diagrams of the principal relationships in pre-production.)

Getting a Slot

An agent's reputation rests in part with their ability to present casting directors and their clients with actors who are competent, professional and right for the roles being cast. When an agent receives a breakdown, he submits names and/or headshots of those he thinks are best suited to the available roles. Whether or not you are included may depend on a number of factors. Among them:

- how many people are being seen (or how many slots the agency has been allotted)
- whether you have the ability and/or experience to perform the role
- whether an agent or casting director considers you right for the role
- how many actors like you a particular agent represents
- whether your preference with this casting director is with this agency
- whether you are exclusive with this agency in that category

et cetera, et cetera, et cetera.

Due to the nature of the advertising industry, those casting commercials are frequently more willing to look at newer talent, so if an agent has confidence in you and you're right for the role, it's often easier to get you seen. "I'm never adverse to seeing new performers," says Charlotte-based director Bob Newcomb. "But I'll also request performers I've had good experiences with in the past."

Film & television auditions are frequently reserved for actors with more experience under their belt, and as such are sometimes harder to come by. Part of the partnership with your agent involves trusting their ability to determine whether you should be submitted. If you are seen too early for a role that's beyond your present capabilities, you could damage your relationship with the casting director to the degree that they won't be interested in seeing you a second time. "I rarely send new people on a long-shot job," says Linda Newcomb of JTA. "It's just too risky," Virginia agent Marsha Wulf concurs. "It's unfair to the novice to be put out there by an agent, competing against people who have a tremendous amount of training and experience." The solution is to make sure your agent knows at what level you're working — through showcases and plays, classes you're involved in, etc. — and trust that word of your good work will spread.

If you're auditioning on a regular basis but still have not booked a job, your natural reaction may be to wonder what you're doing wrong. Chances are, nothing. "It takes 1 to 2 years to get established, and I define that as when you begin to be requested by producers and casting directors. It may take four or more years to land one network commercial," advises agency owner Rona Burns. "But you know you're doing well when the ratio of callbacks to auditions is better than 50%." Try to avoid the tendency to second-guess the process, or you may end up suppressing the very part of yourself that you're being called-in for in the first place. Just keep working out in your classes and groups to keep your auditions fresh. "The measuring stick is if you're being requested," Linda Newcomb affirms.

Have patience, your agent is on your side.

On Auditioning

Make the role yours. Don't worry about what you think they are looking for — show them how the role will be played if they cast you.

JUANELL WALKER, TALENT TREK AGENCY

We're not going to try to instruct you in the art of the audition. We continue to encourage you to learn that in a class designed specifically for that purpose. However, once you are familiar with the audition and callback process, there are some tips and observations collected from agents, casting directors, producers and directors that you may want to keep in mind:

- Always bring two headshots, and have more if they're needed. This was usually the first and most consistent comment.

- Establish a consistent plan or routine for approaching the audition. Arrive early enough to focus, warm-up and complete your preparation without feeling rushed. "Think of an audition as an interruption of your day," says veteran actor and instructor Sylvia Harmon, "and then go on about living your life."

- If you have a chance, adds Sylvia, "Find out who the director/producer is, and what they've done." It can help establish a relationship as something beyond "Hire *me*."

- Be punctual. "Early is on-time, on-time is late." says agent Rona Burns.

- Don't make excuses for why you are late. Nobody cares.

- Don't attend an audition for which you do not have an appointment.

- Respect the job. If you don't want it, don't audition.

- Have the copy or sides memorized. It's OK to keep the paper, but have the lines in your head. Everyone has gone to a great deal of effort to get them to you: memorize the lines.

- Don't chat. The casting director has lots of auditions and only a limited amount of time. If they're chatting fine, otherwise, be pleasant and get down to business.

- Don't schmooze. Trying to make friends with the director or producer, or otherwise indulge in self-promotional behavior just makes you look like you're insecure about your skill as an actor. "It's simply not your responsibility to do a sales job on the producers in the audition — it doesn't reflect well on you," relates Sally Vaughan, veteran agent and former casting director. "If you're good, you can be quietly confident. But if you push too hard, you can actually ruin your chances of getting the job. Always let your agent do the pushing. Just be friendly."

- When auditioning for the casting director alone (no director, no camera), ask whether they want the reading directed at them or away from them. They all have different preferences. Never incorporate them physically into the reading.

- Ask whatever questions you have before you start. Don't start until you are ready.

- Learn to listen and follow direction. This is crucial and seems so fundamental that it is easily overlooked. Strive to develop your listening and intuitive skills — sometimes hard to come by in the pressure of an audition situation.

- Hold until you are told to cut. Don't stop yourself and ask "How did I do?" or apologize for something you think you did wrong. "It's a clear message that you're not confident," warns Linda Newcomb, "and can compromise your whole audition."

- "Remember that the camera is always rolling," advises Annette Stilwell."When you say things like 'Should I slate?' or 'Which agent am I with today?' it can make you look like an amateur, especially to clients in bigger markets."

- In a callback, do what you did in the first audition. Don't try to outdo what you did the before — you were called back to see if you could do it again. However, "If we give you a note for a callback," says casting director Tracy Kilpatrick, "you should heed our advice. When you don't

do it or do something you think is better, it often makes us look foolish."

"Audition with good work and a good demeanor. Honor the art and respect the client equally whether they're Stephen Spielberg or a first-time director," encourages Linda Newcomb. "And thank them for their time," adds Lisa Fincannon. "It's just common courtesy."

Just Flip the Burgers...

(or...How to Act Your Way Right Out of a Job)

Most professional actors have chosen to remain in this always-competitive, often frustrating, sometimes confusing field because they have an intense love of the art of acting. As professionals, we work extremely hard to perfect and maintain our skills. We take class as often as we can. We read, we watch, we analyze. We know our craft. We are prepared. In the overall scheme of succeeding as an actor, these are good — great — practices.

Standing between you, your training, your commitment and your goal of landing enough paying jobs to earn the right to call yourself a "working actor" however, is one of the trickiest aspects of the business: the audition. Finding the proper balance between honesty and technique, preparation and performance, thinking and doing is a skill that we, as actors, should never underestimate.

Consider the following story:

The project was a national commercial. It involved different scenarios of people cooking hamburgers and things that go wrong in the process. A comedy — a high-paying comedy. The casting director felt there were two great prospects for the available roles.

The first had recently attended a workshop by a high-powered, out-of-town professional. In her zeal to put the points that had been touched upon in this expensive workshop to good use, the actress infused the simple scene with an abundance of misdirected busywork. In doing so, she muddied her performance, forfeited all spontaneity, and lost the job.

The second actor was the casting director's first choice. This was a callback by now, so the actor should have known what to do. Still, he shifted his weight back and forth, knitting his brow as if trying to work out some monumental problem.

"What's wrong," the casting director asked. "How can I help?"

"I'm not sure of my motivation," said the actor.

The clients, who were sitting at the casting table, heard the exchange.

"Hunger," one of them called out, snickering.

While this comment was obviously disrespectful to the actor, the client made a valid point. From his side of the table, the actor's performance needs to appear effortless. In the end, this actor got in his own way by over-thinking what should have been obvious. Needless to say he didn't get the job either.

The appearance of effortlessness is of key importance to any audition. The point is not to try to impress them with your prowess as an actor, or to help them appreciate how hard you are working or how difficult your job is. The point is...to flip the burgers. The trick is that at the same time, you need to flip the burgers believably, honestly and with a sense that there is a real person attached to the arm doing the flipping.

We are not trying to negate the importance of careful and complete preparation for any audition you may be invited to (or any job you might land, for that matter). But, regardless of whether it's a heavy feature film or a fast food commercial, the last thing the client or casting director wants to see in an audition is your preparation or your technique. Of course, you need to understand the script — if there is one. Of course, you need to fill in the blanks, to make choices. Of course, you need to prepare. Then you need to leave that preparation in the waiting room and flip the burgers!

So...focus on doing your job rather than getting the job. Putting your focus on doing your job will minimize the fear factor and release you from the feeling of having to please everybody or impress anybody. In addition, here are some final tips to concentrate on before entering the audition space...

1. Be certain you are emotionally prepared to behave in a friendly and professional manner. (This implies leaving your

day job hassles, the fact that you haven't worked in a month and any other miscellaneous baggage at the door.) "A professional can always focus," notes actor Rodney Pickel.

2. Be certain you know the facts: why you are there, who you are supposed to see and what the project is. If you are auditioning for a commercial, be certain you know — and can correctly pronounce — the client's name and/or the subject of the spot. (Your agent should give you this information.)

3. If you have been given a script ahead of time, be certain you have read it OUT LOUD. (We cannot tell you the number of actors who have bumbled simply because they waited until they were in the audition to actually speak the words.) If you are not given a script prior to the audition, ask to see one once you have signed in and find a quiet place to read it OUT LOUD.

4. Answer the basic questions of who, where, what and why. From these choices, develop a clear moment before so that the character has a life before the scene begins. Keep these active. Keep these simple. (If you do not know how to find the answers to the above, enroll in a good acting class ASAP.)

5. Having done your homework, take a deep breath and put your attention where it belongs: on "being awake in the moment." Then forget your prep and...*flip the burgers.*

Trust the casting director — he/she wants you to succeed!

I'll never forget casting for a video store manager whose only action was to walk into the store, turn on the lights and throw a switch to power up a wall of TV sets. Hey, nothing to it...piece of cake! It was a principal role that could have been cast from headshots. Several guys dutifully walked through the improv effortlessly. Any of them would have been perfect.

Finally, the last actor came in, took a minute to focus and then proceeded to take me on a journey of a prideful manager coming to work at the crack of dawn, ducking from the chill hitting the imaginary switch and lighting up the room. The improv resonated with such authenticity that it lit up his eyes and my heart. He didn't overshoot, nor did he phone-in his performance. He simply executed a clear intention with enough emotional investment to convince me this character was real and had a life. He won the part.

DIRECTOR GEORGE WATKINS

Staying Afloat

That Desperate Feeling

So many actors — their talent notwithstanding — seek in this profession something they can never obtain. It leads them to obsess on the work, compromise themselves and others, and leave them highly vulnerable to the constant rejection and industry frauds with promises galore. Only you know if you are one of them. The signs? A pit in your stomach anytime you hear of an audition for which you weren't called. Not being able to talk about anything else, to anyone. Participating in gossip and negativity among actors in waiting rooms and casual conversation. Always looking for something to change (your look, your headshot, your agent) so They'll pick you, constantly trying to figure out what They want. Asking fellow actors if they have been busy and having your heart sink when they say yes (even if they mean renovating the basement). Hesitating to refer other actors for potential roles because you're afraid they'll be better than you.

Because there is so much that is out of your control, there is an inherent insecurity in the pursuit of this work. If you sought it to obtain outside validation, even subconsciously, you are in for a long and brutal struggle. "Desperation grows, shows and feeds on itself," says former agent Judy Cook. If it's inside you, it's in the audition, and it's likely the very thing that's keeping you from what you want. So how do you counter it?

"**Have something else that matters to you,**" emphasizes Judy Cook. Is it your kids' soccer games? Researching family genealogy? Revitalizing your garden? Singing in the church choir? Learning Japanese? Volunteering at the shelter? Studying the Kabala? Renewing your interest in interior design? Pick something that will nourish your creativity and bring its own inherent reward. "Actors can't possibly bring anything new to their work unless they are experiencing life," emphasizes Tommy Housworth. After all, it's what we are paid to portray.

Understand what is out of your control. The more you can appreciate the million and one factors that determine who is cast and who is not, the less you will take it personally when it is not you. Profound disappointment is one thing, but you must find a way to counter the what-did-I-do-wrong response. Remember that every actor — however successful — has felt it, experienced it and sometimes been overcome by it. The difference is that some learn how to cope with it, and some do not. "I've actually heard some actors speak as if there was a conspiracy against them," recounts actor Tommy Housworth. "If you've never been on the other side of the casting table, I encourage you to discover how hard it is: the decision making process is so often contingent upon some intangible thing. Believe me, those doing the casting WANT you to succeed! They want you to be the one they are looking for!" The problem is, they cannot cast us all.

It's such a fickle business. Anytime you get a job, all you know is that it's going to end one day. You can't put all your eggs in one basket — you have to be prepared.

Actor Kathy Payne

Find the one who loves you and doesn't know beans from acting. Pets are perfect for this. "What's a movie? Com'on, throw the *ball*! " Moms, real friends and kids are also good choices. A vital therapeutic or spiritual group can usually lend a steadying hand, and will always clue you in when your perspective is teetering out of balance. We also know of a group of actors in Atlanta that meets for breakfast regularly. They're all in the business and sometimes compete for roles, but they do not discuss bookings or auditions or jobs. Instead, they share all the other parts of their lives among them: travels, hobbies, families, along with the common frustrations of the business.

Have some other source of income, at least in the beginning. It will keep you from compromising yourself and your career right down to your last self-denigrating bone ("I have to pay the rent, don't I?"). This is the only industry we know of where part of your job is looking for work. The only problem is, nobody pays you for that part. "There was a time I would do plays for gas money. I was single and I could live on $7000 a year," says Charlotte-based actor Rebecca Koon. "But now my lifestyle is very different, I have a home, children... No matter how successful you are, the slump is inevitable."

The classic alternative employment is waiting tables and temp work, but there are many ways to support yourself other than by taking work you can't abide or you feel doesn't serve you. One agent speaks of an actor she represents who offers window washing and other services for wealthy clients. "He even hires other actors!" she says. Other employment possibilities include sales, carpentry and home renovation, tennis and golf pro positions, graphic arts and web design. Start with who you are when you not acting, as Judith said, and see what kind of supplemental income that might lead to. (You might even write a book!)

Expand your perspective. Just as working as a stand-in will give you insight into how a film set operates, offering to help out in an agent's office temporarily or periodically will afford you an incredible insight into a entirely different perspective of the business. Likewise for casting sessions — frequently they could use an assistant to run camera (you need to be proficient, however). The insight you gain by putting yourself in another role (and helping out in the meantime) can be immeasurable.

Take control of what you can. This will consist primarily of two things: your work, and what goes on inside of you. We all like to get hired, but very likely there is a reason you got involved in this work that's beyond the monetary one. Reconnect with that and find a way to do it whether it pays or not. Do a showcase with a scene by a favorite writer, get involved in stagework, or start writing that screenplay you keep talking about. "I was doing improv children's theatre and working a comedy act when Spike Lee asked me if I wanted to do *School Days*," recalls Bill Nunn. "Good things happen when you're doin' stuff."

If you need therapy, get therapy. Actors by nature have an overwhelming desire to connect through their art with the world and all the humanity it holds. This desire is rarely validated in The World At Large, and it's sometimes difficult to maintain any sense of it for yourself. It can make you feel crazy, act crazy, and be extremely vulnerable to whoever and whatever supports you in that choice. It's so easy to become consumed by the desire to be stroked, to be chosen; risking unhealthy dependence on those who feed it to you and losing the capacity to effectively evaluate anything about yourself, your work or your life. Examples of this might be a romantic involvement with an acting coach who is amazed at the deep work you do; or being tempted by an offer from the charlatan holding a too-private audition in a remote motel room; feeling alive only in acting classes where emotional intensity is the norm; and giving yourself away by taking demeaning roles in projects that have no intrinsic value whatsoever.

"Acting can be therapeutic, but it's not therapy. Those who eat, drink, and breathe it can burn out," says writer/actor Tommy Housworth. "Balance is important. Take it seriously, but don't use it to fill voids in other areas of your life."

What do you do when you don't get the role (after the *third* callback...)?

Jill Jane Clements	"I take to my bed."
Stuart Culpepper	"I squeeze my grandson . . . a LOT."
Robin O'Dell	"I just tell myself, oh well, their loss."
Shannon Eubanks	"I get totally depressed...It used to last for weeks, but now it only lasts about half an hour."
Terry Loughlin	"I've just learned how to forget about it."
Steve Coulter	"I try to trust the Big Plan... there may be some more important reasons why I wasn't cast that I don't understand now. So I just sit down and wait 'til it stops hurting."
Della Cole	"I try to remember that this is just somebody else's time . . . which means it'll be my time later."
Kathy Payne	"I make sure I've got plans immediately after the callback so that it doesn't become the most important thing of the day."
Margo Moorer	"I trust that God has a reason. For example, I really wanted to play an African, and I was *extremely* upset when I didn't get cast in *The Patriot.* Now I have a 6-year contract with Corsica Productions, playing Kali, an African."

Short Subjects

That's My Kid!

OK honey, do what the nice man says...

We went to several reputable kids' agents and asked them what they might like us to pass on to parents of potential child actors. Without exception, their first response was this: Parents MUST be honest with themselves about who it is that wants to be on-camera. If the desire to pursue this work is not entirely the child's own, it is a complete waste of everyone's time — not to mention a precious childhood. "I've become pretty adept about knowing right away who would really love to be in show business..." says agency owner Jackie Pressley. "The parent or the child."

It is only natural for you as a parent to see your child's uniqueness and charm — perhaps others have commented on these qualities — but the truth is that this business requires an incredible amount of patience, commitment, discipline and sacrifice from both children and their parents. "I get so many calls from parents who just KNOW their child is the most beautiful, the most talented — sure they have the next McCauley Culkin," Jackie adds. But no amount of lighting or makeup can hide the look in a child's eyes if he'd rather be hanging with his buds than sitting under hot lights for hours waiting to say "Oh, boy!" for the thirtieth time, with just a little more enthusiasm, OK? This is assuming, of course, that this same look has not surfaced more than a couple of times during the twenty or so other auditions he had before he booked this part — one of the two or three parts he is likely to get this year, if he does well. If all that is not going to be Big Fun to your child, there is not a single reason to consider it.

Every casting director to whom we spoke recounted heart-breaking stories of "stage parents" in the waiting room, begging, cajoling and even threatening children who for

> *If I call with an audition and your child would rather play in their soccer game or attend a friend's birthday party, then I want them to do that. A child's first "job" is to be a child.*
>
> JACKIE PRESSLEY
> OWNER/AGENT, CAI KIDS

Many times a parent refuses to listen to an honest evalu-ation of a child's audition or interview. We've had parents become irate when told their child was simply not ready. They insist their child is a genius at home in front of the camera. This may be true, but if he can't share that talent to the people conducting the interview, he'll likely have his most promising career in home movies.

FROM **The Actor's Guide for Kids**
BY JEN KELLEY AND BRENDA KROCHMAL

whatever reason would simply rather be doing something else. "I've actually seen parents bribing kids to audition," reports Linda Higgs of Moore-Higgs Casting. "How good could that audition possibly be?" Florida casting director Kimberly Mullen concurs. "It's pointless — you lose the essence of the child." One casting director even reported counseling a client not to use a delightful child because of the impossible behavior she had witnessed toward the child by her father during the audition. "I can't bear to see a parent exhibiting anything remotely resembling force or abuse towards their child," says casting director Lori Wyman, "if I see it, I will never call them in for an audition again."

Ask yourself the following questions. What is your child's temperament around unfamiliar people? Is he shy, ill-at-ease or easily upset? Does she show off and become out-of-control?

(We're looking for natural, spontaneous self-expression, not "Mommy watch me.") Can he (and you) tolerate long periods of waiting, at auditions or on the set, without becoming fussy? Is he disciplined? Or, as Kathy Hardegree of Atlanta Models & Talent puts it, "Does he mind?" Can he follow direction — yours, and others? Keep in mind that if the child is over three, the parent will likely not be allowed in the audition or on the set during the shoot. Could your child adapt? You must understand that the desired behavior can never be coaxed or forced out of a child.

A wonderful way to explore a child's natural interest and apti-tude for acting is through some of the theatrical and other professional training programs available (in our directory, youth training will be noted in the description). These classes will introduce your child to both the fun and the work involved — and will give both of you an idea of whether it's just a diver-sion or something he might like to pursue more seriously. Advises kids' instructor Lisina Longo, "Just don't fall into the trap of thinking it's all about the job. A good training program will be more about real acting techniques and your child as an individual, while incorporating the basic on-camera, on set, and on stage skills they'll need to compete."

Most parents think that this is an easy business. They have no idea what they are getting into.

JACKIE PRESSLEY, CAI KIDS

Audit and compare several programs before you make your choice. Once classes begin, you'll quickly begin to gather a variety of information from instructors and parents whose kids who may be working already. And in the eyes of a prospective agent, it could only help for him to see you're both serious enough to be preparing on your own and will not be relying totally on him to educate you. Moreover, several agents we spoke to mentioned that kids that had some experience in the theatre seemed to have an edge when it came to on-camera work. This could involve participation in anything from school plays to community and regional theatre productions.

Agents, the Kids and You

To approach an agent initially, all you need is one good, natural photograph or full body shot of your child. These may be taken by a professional photographer, or you may take them yourself, so long as they are simple, clean and representative of your child's personality. The emphasis here is on natural — glamour for a child is only appropriate in a beauty pageant. (An appropriate beauty pageant — there's an oxymoron.) Check commercials and magazine ads. Any lipstick or mascara you see will be doing its best not to look like make-up. It's real kids we want, not miniature Barbie and Ken dolls.

Accuracy is also important in a child's headshot. If there are braces in the picture, there'd better be braces on the kid, and vice versa. Because your child is growing and changing so quickly, it is important that you keep up by using the most recent pictures you can. Why? Let's say I'm your agent. I get a call for six year-old girls with short, curly-blond hair. My pictures of little Stephanie say this is so, so I submit her, and she gets the audition. But when I call, Mom tells me that no, Stephanie now sports long, flowing tresses that have darkened quite a bit (and she turned seven last month). So I have to let the my client know that no, they won't be seeing Stephanie. You have wasted a lot of my time and effort and caused me embarrassment with my client. What will I think of the next time I consider submitting little Stephanie?

When your child has reached the age of five or so, you may want to have a professional headshot taken. Your child will not be changing as drastically as he was in earlier years, so a professional headshot becomes a more sensible investment. Don't waste money having a composite card made (several photographs with different looks on one card, used primarily for commercial print) until you are signed by an agent and they

---

I look for a child who is open, personable, and can conduct himself well in the room. Often times I'll give him a script to perform as a cold reading. If he is very young, I'll ask him to repeat a few lines to see if he can take direction. For children about nine years and older, I'll ask them in advance to prepare a monologue for the audition.

JEN KELLEY, AGENT, PEOPLE STORE

can advise you — they'll most likely have you redo them anyway. Reread the section entitled 'Approaching an Agent' for guidelines on contacting an agent initially.

Once your child is signed, it's important to understand that you and your agent are now in partnership. If you and your child hold up your end of the bargain, it could only increase your child's opportunities over others whose lack of professionalism creates work for agents who are likely already inundated. For instance:

- You and your child should be available for auditions as much as possible whenever they occur, sometimes on very short notice. Your agent has very little control over the audition schedule and can rarely adjust it to yours or your child's. This includes band, cheerleading, and basketball practice, as well as your hair appointment which takes three weeks to schedule.

- You can also expect that your child will have to be out of school if he is booked, so you'll need to check with them to see if these types of absences will be excused.

- If an agent has taken the time to get the copies of the **sides** (portions of script) to you prior to the audition, he expects the child to be familiar with them when he comes in to read. If you see that your child resists taking the time to do so, it could be time to re-evaluate his overall interest in doing this work.

- And of course, keep plenty of accurate, up-to-date head-shots on-hand for agents.

It's also important not to forget the amount of rejection that is inherent in this business, even in a successful career. It's one of the most difficult things for an adult actor to endure — and it will be absolutely critical that you understand how to help your child deal with it. Both of you must understand that's it's never anybody's "fault" when she's not cast. If she auditions and has fun doing it, she's done her job.

And what if, after all the initial hard work and sacrifice, your child is actually offered a rare opportunity in a film or television series? Rebecca Shrager tells of a young man who was cast in a primary role in a film and was booked for five weeks of shooting at an out-of-town location. His mother had to leave her job in order to be with him during the shoot. Keep in mind that no matter what success this young man might enjoy as a result of this film, there was no guarantee there would be another role of this kind for him. Is this level of sacrifice acceptable to you should your child become the kind of success for which you've both struggled?

Most clients want kids to just be kids. Agents work so hard getting them to slate correctly and stand on their mark. They seem fake, like little robots. Just teach children to have respect for the elders in the room and have fun instead of trying to do everything "right".

Paige Johnston, Corrigan & Johnston Casting

One more word of warning: if there's anyone more vulnerable to unprincipled agents than an unwitting, inexperienced actor, it's an unwitting, inexperienced parent of a child actor. A parent dedicated to affording his or her child with every possible opportunity to fulfill their dream is a prime target for the most unscrupulous in this business. Read and re-read the first chapter in this book. Cash outlay, especially up-front, has absolutely no correlation to increasing the likelihood of success for your child. Everything you need, from training to headshots, is available at reasonable — not heart-stopping — cost, and is never paid to individuals to represent you, such as an agent. Take your time. Investigate several opportunities for training and orientation. If the sales job seems just a little too intense, or if there is some connection between your purchasing anything and whether or not your child will be represented, keep moving. Package sales are very likely the primary income source of that organization, not commission from talent work.

An excellent resource of information is **The Young Performer's Handbook**, published by AFTRA/SAG and available from any SAG office.

You Should Do Voice-over!

You have a great voice. . .

You walk into a studio for your first thirty-second television commercial voice-over spot.

You greet the ad agency representatives, their clients (whose product is being advertised) and the sound engineer. Your handed the script, or copy (it's the first time you've seen it) and the engineer whisks you away to the recording booth. "Did you want to stand or sit?" Well, you're not really sure.

You should be. From this moment on, every word, every breath, every sign, every sound you make can be heard by the roomful of people staring at you through the glass window of this tiny, silent room which is your domain. For the next hour or so, all eyes and ears are on you: The One Who Will Fulfill All Expectations.

All communication is done through your headset, but you'll hear them only when they want you to. The sound engineer asks you to read the copy so he can set the proper audio levels. This is your first chance to practice before recording actually begins — you have less than a minute. Gosh, your breathing seems loud...you sound like Darth Vader or an obscene phone-caller. Can they hear that? [yes.] "Okay, we're set. Whenever you're ready."

Take 1..."Uhh, that was good," the director says, "but you need to speed it up quite a bit. We're over about ten seconds." Oka-a-y, ten seconds...wow. How much faster should I — "Ready?" [no.] "Here we go."

Take 2...No immediate response, but they're all talking animatedly together and they're...they're laughing! What's so funny?... "Uh, sorry." Huh? Oh, it's the director... "We were okay on time but it sounded a little rushed in spots. So start off at the same pace you were last time and then slow down a bit on the third line. Throw away the next two lines and then billboard the product name and that should do it." Throw what?

VOICE-OVER:

1. The voice of an off-camera narrator, announcer, or actor.

2. A recorded, broadcast or televised sequence (as in a commercial) using such a voice.

Take 3...Got tongue-tied and flubbed up. It happens. But it better not happen too often.

Take 4...Darn! I didn't — "We still need more emphasis on the product name..." Right, right.

Take 5...Perfect! Except you popped your Ps.

Take 6...About a second too fast.

Take 7...A second too slow.

Take 8...Technical difficulty, not your fault.

Take 9...Someone didn't like the way you said "specific."

Take 10... Whoops! Frog in your throat.

Take 11...Why are they taking so long...?

Finally. "Listen, we're almost there, but we're losing the energy and excitement of the piece. We don't want it to sound rushed, so give us the energy but relax and flow with it, okay?...Oh, and try something different with the word 'bountiful.' We wanna feel the bounty — but don't take too much time with it or we'll be over. Okay. Just relax and let's go with it. This is the one." O-ka-a-ay. Let's see, energy but not rushed. Don't pop the Ps. Watch out for "specific." Do something with "bountiful." Slow down on the third line...but not too much! Throw away the next two lines... What else? Oh yeah, don't forget to billboard the product! And...and...and...Rela-a-a-x!

So...still wanna do voice-overs? Well of course you do — you and everybody else we know. The truth is, the world of voice-over is even more competitive than the world of acting, with most of the work being done by a very small percentage of talented folks whose skills include much more than just "a good voice." "Voice-acting is the most difficult of all," according to Stuart Culpepper, Atlanta-based actor and voice talent. "Your voice has to do it all. You can't hide behind your charming smile, your captivating expression, your fabulous costume or flattering hairstyle." A television commercial voice-over session can take as many as fifty takes, or until you get it exactly the way the client wants it: stress here, nuance there, a certain "feel" they may — or may not be able to communicate. You'll be expected to respond to any type of direction: from a specific line reading, to the vague and enigmatic "So...anything different you'd like to try?" Your voice is the crowning addition to a project involving countless people, and many thousands of dollars. Ultimately it is you — your voice, and your ability to use it effectively — that is speaking for their product, so a lot is riding on you. Can't wait, right? Okay, let's get started.

Voice-over Venues

When we think voice-over, we immediately think of television and radio commercials. But there are many other types of voice-over: narration for corporate sales, documentaries, point-of-purchase, CD-ROM, voice mail, animation voice-overs...the list goes on and on. That's the good news. And as technology keeps expanding, there is a constantly increasing demand for more of every kind of voice-over. New kinds of applications are springing up every year, which translates into nice work...if you can get it. So if you even think you could be one of the lucky few who do it for a living, you'd be crazy not to try.

What Do You Need?

Like newscasting, the bulk of the work is accent-free, so you must be able to lose every trace of any accent unless it is called for specifically. Let's say you have a reliable, clear, pleasant and/or interesting speaking voice, and good enunciation. That's a start; you have the minimum requirements. "It's not just the kind of voice you have, it's what you can do with the voice that's important," emphasizes voice-expert Judith Sullivan. But you'll also need excellent cold-reading skills (the ability to read copy, sight-unseen, and not sound as if you are reading). Beyond that, it's important to understand the copywriter's intent, so that you can help convey that in your read. And you'll need to have strong, highly-flexible interpretation skills, to help you follow through on any direction given. Sounds like acting, doesn't it? Well, it is. And like film acting and commercial work, you'll have to repeat the same thing, take after take, until every person on the other side of that glass is satisfied that they've gotten what they wanted. Just because there's no camera, don't underestimate the amount of pressure.

So What Comes First?

The best way to begin acquiring these skills and test yourself in a risk-free environment, is to either enroll in a voice-over workshop or enlist the help of a private coach (see the "Training: Voice/Voice-over" listings in the directory). There's a lot more to the voice-over profession than can be learned on your own or from any book. The information and feedback you'll receive from experienced instructors is invaluable, and your first professional job will probably pay for the class. "Don't rush out to the studio to do a demo," says Paul Armbruster, voice talent and instructor. "Get some coaching first. Even if you have a real flair for doing this you need some more honing of those skills before you do a demo."

And if you're not doing it already, start listening very closely to the voices on television and radio commercials. Try to determine what makes them tick...or not. Repeat various lines from the best for practice. Whenever you get the chance, read

---

Being a voice talent is the same as being an on-camera talent. You have to be good at what you do, and you have to compile the appropriate promotional materials. A professional voice demo is as essential for voice-over as a headshot is for on-camera work.

SALLY VAUGHAN, VOICE-OVER AGENT, PEOPLE STORE

aloud from books, magazines, etc. Work with actual voice-over copy from friends in the business, or transcribe your own from television, radio or even magazine ads, accumulating the best copy as you go. When you begin to feel confident that you could actually be comfortable in that tiny, silent booth, you're ready for the next step.

The Demo

The principal calling-card in voice-over is known as the Voice-over Demo. This is a CD or cassette copy of about 10 to 20 pieces of various commercials all strung together like one long, stunning two-minute advertisement of your various vocal styles and capabilities. "It doesn't matter how long it is, it's how long it seems," says Judith Sullivan. Producing a demo is a tedious, pains-taking and costly process, but it is as essential to a voice talent as a headshot and resume are to an actor.

The Producer

Before we continue with the how-to of voice-demo production, we'd like to offer three pieces of sage advice:

Hire a producer. Hire a producer. Hire a producer.

They are not cheap — you pay them by the hour. But they are the substitute for your inexperience and lack of objectivity, which in our opinion makes them pretty close to priceless. They'll advise you on copy selection and assist in its prepara-

tion; they'll be invaluable during the actual recording session and mixing process; and they'll throw in an unlimited supply of moral support free of charge. Yes, we know, we're talking real money here. Just remember: an effective demo and the ability to back it up is crucial to your marketability as voice talent. In fact, a significant amount of voice-over work is booked directly from your demo without an audition, so every hour and dollar spent will be more than worth it. If you don't have the money, save it. If don't want to spend it, you might want to think about changing careers.

"Some people say, 'I gotta start somewhere...' But you can't, not anymore," says agency owner Kathy Hardegree. "For voice talent, there's no longer only a 'local' or 'regional' market. With today's technology, a voice talent with access to the right equipment can be recorded from practically anywhere. You're competing against top national talent right from the start."

Check with your agent or workshop instructor. He or she may be available to produce your demo, or recommend someone who can.

Preparing to Record

With or without a producer, begin by listening to as many different demos as you can: in your workshop sessions, from your agent, friends in the business, or visit a sound studio and ask to listen to their collection. "Listen to house reels from talent agencies in New York and L.A. (voicebank.net is a good source) before you record your demo," encourages actor and voice-talent Wilbur Fitzgerald. "Having a professional CD demo is more important than it's ever been." Become familiar with other voices in the market with which you'll be competing. Don't listen with the intention of copying anyone, but do notice what you like about them: the voice, the copy, the different types of spots, the style in which they're produced.

The next step is copy selection. From the treasure trove you've been gathering, choose the fifteen or so which work best for you, based on the following criteria:

- it has not been used on other demos

- it's interesting, not mundane or run-of-the-mill

- it's not a widely-known national spot, or currently-running local spot

- it lends itself to your 'style,' which will have been determined in your workshop. For example, top voice-talent Jeff Winter calls this his "bread-and-butter voice." The tag that describes it is on his business card and his web site: *Taking Voice-over to Heart*. You don't even have to hear it, do you?

"And find something funny," Judith Sullivan adds. "Everybody wants to laugh. And include at least one dialog spot if you're good at it." They're very popular and it's important to represent that type of skill on your demo.

The two most important things are that you sound great delivering the spots, and you are able to recreate their style effortlessy in a session. Don't worry that they're not authentic commercials — many of the top national talents use these fabricated spots as a way to demonstrate their capabilities and round out their presentation. "You should be really comfortable with what's on your tape," advises Jeff Winter, and completely capable of duplicating any style on your demo with minimal direction once you're hired. "Your demo is a promise," adds Marice Tobias, a Los Angeles-based producer/instructor. "It tells someone what kind of a time they're going to have when they work with you." If you can't make good on your "promise" when you walk into the studio, you probably won't get a second chance.

After determining which copy works best for you, edit each one down to it's essential ten to fifteen seconds. Studio time is bought by the hour. Don't waste money recording the full spots (if you've done your homework, you'll know full spots aren't used on any demo). Recording at least fifteen different pieces so you can pick the very best ones for your final demo.

The Recording Session

When you're at last ready to record, contact the studio you've selected (see guidelines in the Recording Studios section of the directory) and request time for a voice demo recording session of at least two to three hours. Most major studios have a reduced fee for voice-over talent.

Mixing the Final Version

If you're not using a producer, leave the studio session with a cassette or CD copy of all your good 'takes' so you can listen to them once you're back home (and off the clock). Select the best ones to be edited together for the final version of each spot. For example, you and your producer) may prefer the first line from take one and the last two lines from take ten. Be sure to take specific notes — you want to pay the sound engineer for his audio expertise, not for his ability to search for that one take you know is on there somewhere...

When you return to the studio, the engineer will mix your selected takes, adjusting sound levels and tone quality, adding sound effects and music, magically making them indistinguishable from real commercials. This process can take several hours (you don't need to be there), so ask for an approximate estimate, allowing an hour margin. Be conscious of the order in which you'd like the spots to occur on the demo — this is more critical than you might think. Paul Armbruster emphasizes that "It's well-nigh impossible to order the spots without producing (or mixing) them first." He recommends repeating the same procedure you followed for the unedited takes: leave the studio the second time with a cassette copy of the individually mixed spots, listen at home, and try out various combinations using your dual cassette deck. "Music and sound effects can completely alter the feel of a spot," Paul adds.

Some notes about music: Many studios charge up to $100 for each music selection, or bed, used (it's because they're charged for it) so try to find a studio whose hourly rate includes everything, or one that at least has a reduced rate for music usage. You can give the engineer an idea of what you want for each segment (particular sound effects, 'bubbly' or 'romantic' music, etc.), or you can leave it all up to them. If you're particularly confident, you can even bring in your own music selections to help offset any music charges (CD only).

Copies for Distribution

Once the final mix is complete, you'll return to the studio one last time to listen to your finished demo with the engineer and make any minor changes. You'll then be given a master copy on either DAT (Digital Audio Tape) or CD from which you'll make copies for agents and clients. Before then however, Wilbur Fitzgerald adds one final word of caution. "Listen to three or four other demos along with yours. If it doesn't compare, wait." If you still need more polish to compete effectively, it will be in your best interest even now to acquire the skills you lack before presenting them to others.

To have audio cassette (gradually becoming a dinosaur) or CD copies made, get dub (duplication) house recommendations from your producer, or look in the yellow pages under Tape or

Media Duplication. Get several estimates before proceeding. It's also important to have a professional presentation, so both a high-quality dub and a printed label on the cassette/CD are essential. "Your demo should have at minimum labels, j-cards and cases…otherwise you appear less than professional," says agent Sally Vaughan. Offer one demo to each talent agency for their consideration, following the same guidelines for submitting a headshot.

As you can see, just as in acting, there's no small amount of effort involved in pursuing voice-over work. But if you can get a demo that you're happy with, and an agent who likes it — you're well on your way. So off you go. And remember, *relax…*

Come On Over to My House, My House

Face it, the Southeast is a great place to live. The climate is temperate, the pace a little slower and the scenery breathtaking. You can make a decent living as an actor if you're flexible, have something to offer, are willing to travel and can hang in long enough to get established.

Each part of the region has its own particular character and work emphasis. The best market for film may be central and south Florida, where almost fifty local film offices beckon commercials and movies-of-the-week to abandon frigid Canadian winters for kinder, gentler Florida temps. That being said, 1999 was South Carolina's best film year on record. The voice-over market is much stronger in Atlanta, where there is also a great deal of non-broadcast work, with Charlotte and Nashville having their share as well. And of course, Nashville has the bulk of music video production. All the states in the region are continuing to aggressively market the rich geography, history and variety of locations the Southeast has to offer.

Although some revenues are down from when we last reported them in 1990, the amount and type of work varies tremendously throughout the region from year to year and season to season. The economic climate continues to be strong however, with millions of dollars in revenues being pumped into the economy of each individual state.

Good training and diligence are pretty much the standard in the industry wherever you decide to settle, but in the Southeast, you can also take advantage of a rich cultural history. With architecture ranging from ante-bellum to cosmopolitan, geography ranging from mountains to beaches and arts opportunities ranging from country music to fine art, the South is as diverse as the people who live here.

Should you decide to relocate either within the Southeast, or from another region altogether, we suggest you contact the state or local chamber of commerce for travel and relocation information (the directory has a partial listing). In the meantime, here's an overview of each state to get you started:

Alabama

At a glance...
Population (1999): 4.36 million
State capital: Montgomery
Largest city: Birmingham
Industry hotspot: Mobile & Birmingham
Strength: access to Atlanta as well as Nashville and Memphis
1999 Film Revenues: $30.8 million

Nicknamed the Heart of Dixie, Alabama's great variety of locations makes it attractive to film and television producers. Alabama boasts the whole spectrum from the historical southern architecture of Montgomery to shiny, metropolitan Birmingham to Huntsville's technologically advanced space and rocket industry. In the past year, Northern Alabama has seen a good deal of activity in the music video industry spilling over from Nashville. The state has also seen growth in the corporate venue.

Florida

At a glance...
Population (1999): 15.1 Million
State capital: Tallahassee
Largest cities: Miami/Fort Lauderdale, Tampa, Orlando, Jacksonville
Industry hotspots: Miami, Orlando, Tampa

1999 Film Revenues: $3 billion

Strength: Central Florida boasts a strong commercial and seasonal film market, while South Florida is a commercial, print, and modeling stronghold. And there's no income tax.

Florida's year-round temperate climate and variety of lush locations make it a natural choice not only for the tourist, but for film & video production as well. There are two thousand plus miles of shoreline, six hundred of which are beaches which certainly provide glamourous and enticing backgrounds for commercial and print shoots. There's also almost one million square miles of public lands ranging from lakes to forests to everglades. Agriculture that includes orange groves, vineyards and even sugar cane, with thoroughbred farms and race tracks offering additional location choices. And when you consider that Disney and Universal have homes there, along with PaxNet, Telemundo and MTV Latin America, you can understand why production in the state has increased tremendously over the past decade.

Florida has almost fifty local film offices in addition to the central state commission which is one indication of the effort the it has put forth to entice the film industry south. It's divided into two principal regions. Miami/Ft. Lauderdale is the South Florida regional hub, which is considered by many to be the commercial and print capital of the South. Film and television production is year-round, while the commercial season more concentrated in the winter. As one agent told us

"Just watch the weather in New York. A week after it snows there, we'll be flooded with casting calls." Orlando is the focal point for Central Florida, with Tampa holding its own as a developing market.

Georgia

At a glance...
Population (2000): 7.78 million
State capital: Atlanta
Largest cities: Atlanta, Columbus, Savannah, Macon, Albany
Industry hotspot: Atlanta

Film Revenues: $203 million (Film & television projects only. Includes economic impact multiplier, does not include non-broadcast, a major part of the economic picture.)
Strength: Corporate and non-broadcast is the staple in this market, lots of commercial production as well.

The largest state east of the Mississippi River, Georgia's 58,910 square miles have appeared in some 400 feature films during the past 25 years. The state's film commission was established in 1973, and has gone far in promoting the state as a distinctive location for films, television productions, commercials, corporate projects and music videos.

Geographically, the state can be divided into three regions — the mountains to the north, the Piedmont Plateau and the coastal plain. Savannah has established it's own local film commission to assist in representing the surrounding area, which

has enjoyed increased interest as a resulting from the popularity of "Midnight in the Garden of Good and Evil." But the bulk of Georgia's acting opportunities are located in Atlanta, the state capital.

Atlanta sits in the northern part of the state. It is a relatively small city at 132 square miles, but its metropolitan area is one of the largest in the Southeast. The Atlanta region (which includes the city proper as well as the 10 surrounding counties) has seen a recent growth in population which has been matched by rapid economic growth. The city's international reputation was cinched when it was chosen as home for the 1996 Summer Olympics.

As headquarters for some of the largest and best known companies in the U.S. — including Turner Broadcasting System, Coca-Cola and United Parcel Service — it's no wonder that Atlanta has a thriving corporate and commercial industry. The fact that the Georgia's film related activity is rather concentrated makes the state attractive for the actor because you can locate in Atlanta, focus on corporate/commercial work — by far the city's strong suit — but still diversify into the areas of feature films, television, voice-over and print (modeling).

North Carolina

At a glance...
Population (1999): 7.65 million
State capital: Raleigh

Largest city: Charlotte

Industry hotspots: Charlotte, Wilmington (but good work across the state)

1999 Film Revenues: $302 million (real dollars, no multiplier, includes film, television and commercial production)

Strength: fast growing industry with lots of work in every aspect of the business

In 1999 North Carolina hosted 67 major productions, including 22 feature films, 41 television series and mini-series episodes, and 4 Movies-of-the-Week, The state is home to 27 soundstages and seven film production complexes. From the Western region's mountains to Wilmington on the coast, the state's film industry continues to thrive. North Carolina has some of the most varied scenery of any state in the Eastern U.S. To its west are the Blue Ridge Mountains rising close to 6000 feet. In the center of the state are the rolling hills of the Piedmont Plateau (home of cultural and metropolitan meccas such as Charlotte, Raleigh and Greensboro) and the coast is a mix of busy seaports and secluded beachfronts.

For the purposes of the film industry, the state has been divided into seven regions:

Western Region (Asheville and the mountains)

Southeast Region (Wilmington)

Carolinas Region (Charlotte)

Research Triangle Region (Durham)

Piedmont Triad Region (Winston-Salem)

Northeast Region (Outer Banks)

Global TransPark Region

Wilmington is home to EUE Screen Gems Studios, and hosts the bulk of the film/television production. Charlotte, which has seen a tremendous amount of growth in recent years, is strongest in commercial and corporate work. The two cities are located about four hours from each other, so many actors choose to commute back and forth in order to afford themselves the greatest number of audition and work possibilities. In addition, many actors who live in North Carolina choose to commute to Atlanta (which is only four hours from Charlotte) as well as to Virginia and Tennessee.

South Carolina

At a glance...

Population (1999): 3.9 million

State capital: Columbia

Largest cities: Columbia, Charleston, Greenville, Spartanburg

Industry hotspot: Charleston, which is most often used for its location value

1999 Film Revenues: $60.7 million (best year ever for revenues)

Strength: state offers good proximity to both the Atlanta and North Carolina markets

Though not particularly strong in its own right, the South Carolina film and television industry is slowly growing.

Professionals who choose to live in South Carolina (most of those located in Columbia) take advantage of the state's central location. Columbia sits two hours from both Atlanta and Charlotte, two of the hottest spots in the southeastern industry.

The state has a strong tradition of preserving its culture with numerous museums and a variety of collections. A cultural center of the South, Charleston, South Carolina is home to the internationally acclaimed Spoleto Arts Festival. In addition, Charleston's historic architecture makes it a popular location for film and television production.

South Carolina is also noted for its great beach resorts, with Myrtle Beach and Hilton Head Island attracting millions of tourists each year.

Tennessee

At a glance...

Population (1999): 5.48 million

State capital: Nashville

Largest cities: Memphis, Nashville, Knoxville, Chattanooga, Clarksville

Industry hotspots: Memphis & Nashville

1999 Film Revenues: $150 million (does not include music industry)

Strength: music industry which pumped over $4 billion into the state's economy in 1999

While the music business still accounts for the lion's share of the revenues generated by Tennessee's $4.6 billion entertainment industry, film and video production are definitely on the rise. 40 film and television projects were shot in the state in 1996, and several Tennessee based production companies are regularly providing programming to the three major networks. Tennessee's aggressive film commission has worked hard to bring quality productions to the state. The Tennessee-based cable television networks include Home & Garden Television (HGTV), The Food Channel, and the Shop at Home Network.

Nashville, Tennessee is the home of the renowned Grand Ole Opry, the oldest continuous radio show in the United States. If you have musical talent, you may want to consider Opryland or Dollywood, for live stage work, or check out Tennessee's growing music video industry.

Not only is Nashville at the heart of the nation's country music industry, but Tennessee's most important museums are located there, as well as in Memphis. Both cities have also symphonies and Memphis has an opera company as well.

Virginia

At a glance...

Population (1999): 6.87 million

State capital: Richmond

Largest city: Virginia Beach

Industry hotspots: Hampton Roads/Virginia Beach & Norfolk/Richmond

1999 Film Revenues: Virginia: $76 million (up over 115% from 1990)

Strength: good proximity to a variety of markets including Washington DC & North Carolina, great climate

With film revenues continuing to grow every yearly, Virginia's thriving film and video industries have made it an attractive locale for actors. In fact, total direct and indirect income from filming has exceeded $1 billion over the past 20 years!

Technically a mid-Atlantic state, we have chosen to include Virginia in this publication because of the high rate of "talent sharing" between Virginia and the southeast region, North Carolina in particular. The Hampton Roads area, (comprised of several towns that include Virginia Beach, Norfolk, Hampton, Newport News, Williamsburg, and Suffolk) has developed a large and thriving industry centered around cable television production. The centerpiece is New Dominion Pictures which produces numerous reality-based series for the Learning and Discovery Channels including New Detectives, F.B.I Files, and Daring Capers among others. The largest production area in the state, comprising roughly half the crew, actors and pro-duction revenue is found around Richmond. This area tends to host films, mini-series, television movies and commercials and features New Millennium Studios, a full service film studio located in nearby Petersburg. The Washington, D.C. area (comprised of the District, northern Virginia and southern Maryland) is an extremely busy production area, specializing in commercials, documentaries, industrials, corporate and government videos, and some feature film. A few of the many projects that have been filmed in Virginia include Hannibal, Random Hearts, Rules of Engagement, The Contender, Dirty Dancing, What About Bob? and Coal Miner's Daughter.

Virginia can be divided into four geographic regions:

Northern Region

Central Region

Hampton Roads Region

Southwest/Shenandoah Region

A strong supporter of the Arts, Virginia is home to the Virginia Museum of Fine Arts, the country's oldest state-supported museum. The state has a strong tradition in the performing arts with noted companies such as the Barter Theatre in Abingdon; the Virginia Stage Company in Norfolk; Theatre Virginia and Theatre IV in Richmond; Wolf Trap Farm Park for the Performing Arts in Vienna; and Mill Mountain Theatre in Roanoke. Numerous other semi-professional and community theatres are found throughout the state.

California Dreamin'

Well, you've done it. All your work, study and devotion is starting to payoff. You've found an agent you like who really supports you, and you're working fairly regularly: a little theatre, some commercials; you've had a recurring role in a series, and booked quite a few of the features that have come through (with a supporting role in a recent independent). You've got a nice reel, impressive resume. Gee, maybe I should...

Well, you're not alone. You simply couldn't call yourself an actor if you'd never considered a move to the Big Time. There's no question that major roles are cast in major markets, and still the Los Angeles and New York (and maybe Chicago) are still the only places from which nationally recognized careers are launched. But before you give all your plants away...

How to know when to go

We'd love to tell you we had a fool-proof method of determining when and if it was time for you to move on. But like everything else in this business and in most of life, there is none (but you knew that). Finally, it will be your own restlessness that is the key. "If you feel the need to go, you should go," says actor Jim Donadio. Actor and instructor Afemo Omilami concurs. "If you want more you can't stay here. If you are willing to risk all you do have here, then go." In the end, it's not about going or not going...it's about knowing who you are, what you want, and why you want it. Only then will you have the strength and willingness to endure all that you must on the complex journey to who knows where. We're not going to try to talk you out of going, we just want to offer you some things to think about while you're deciding.

You can live here and work or you can live in L.A. and look for an agent.

ACTOR CARL MCINTYRE

Let's assume for our purposes that you are outrageously talented, which you'll need to be to compete at all. "You need to take a good, hard look at what you have to sell," says actor/director/instructor Mike Pniewski, a California native who spent ten successful years in the L.A. market. "First," he says, "you'll need a good, solid demo three to five minutes long." If you don't have it yet, just keep working to you do.

But even that may not count for much. "In L.A. they don't care about your non-union credits. They don't really care about your union credits. If it's not an L.A. credit, it just doesn't count," warns Jim Donadio. Sounds like a catch-22, doesn't it? "However," Jim continues, "anything I can tell you is immediately negated by the 'young' factor, the 'pretty' factor, and the 'luck' factor." Keeping all that in mind, answer the following for yourself:

Are you young? "In Los Angeles particularly over-thirty is over-the-hill," says Kay Butler Hallahan, former agent and talent advisor. "It's especially true if you're a woman. There are already more women for fewer parts," she adds, and the over-thirty women in L.A. are the pros who've already been there for years, with long-time agents and well-cultivated industry relationships. "If you are over 35 and admit it, trying to get an agent on your own is yet another exercise in rejection," Kay advises.

Even if you're a man with years of credits and a variety of experience, don't' expect it to be any easier. "I went to LA in my mid-thirties with an awesome resume and a great reel," relates actor Carl McIntyre. "Every agent I talked to told me they already had me in triplicate."

Are you beautiful? Male or female, beauty is in demand in L.A. "now more than ever, with the talent to back it up," says Kay Hallahan. And we're talking about the heart-stopping, head-turning, skin-deep-not-inner kind of beauty." Reasonably attractive is not even on the chart," Kay adds. What? You've spotted a less-than-gorgeous actor on television? Then we can guarantee that they had a big leg up. Which leads us in turn to ask:

Are you connected? If you're not a stand-up comic who's had your own special on HBO, or don't have an uncle who's an industry pro that can introduce you to the Right People, or haven't figured out yet how to have claimed your fifteen minutes of fame, L.A. is not looking for you. Maybe somebody's seen you, and they like you, and they're in a position to represent you or actually give you work. That sounds great…but be very careful. We know actors all over the region who have left home on the L.A. version of a promise, only to return broke and broken-hearted when it never materialized. After giving up work, selling homes and crossing continents, they were simply brushed aside with the "Right, yeah, hey, ya know, that thing just went away. Crazy business. But good luck, and let us know how it goes!" Click.

But that was *them*, this is *me* . . .

That is exactly what we expected you to say. If you must go, then go. But go prepared. For example:

- **prepare to lay out cash**, and plenty of it. New headshots. Publications. Classes, seminars and showcases — not to mention the everyday cost of living, which in both places can take your breath away. "In New York the apartments are small, the rents high and the fees are rampant," Jim Donadio cautions. "It can cost you 15% of a year's rent to find an apartment through a brokerage agency, which is practically the only way to find what there is available." If you have the option, consider first a temporary move or an extended short stay of three to six months in either place. Give yourself some time to become acclimated and see if it's truly all you expect.

- **prepare for the rejection.** You already know that an actor hears 'no' far more often than 'yes'. Prepare to hear it in every form that it exists, whether or not you eventually hear the 'yes'. "You'll be hard-pressed to find anyone who'll even look at your headshot," says Jim Donadio. "That is, if they don't throw it away right in front of you." If you do get an agent and you don't book in a few auditions, you could find yourself right back looking for a new one.

- **prepare to wait.** This is how Kay Hallanhan puts it: "If you are 22 and look 18, get out of town now...then be pre-

pared to wait A VERY LONG TIME. Every week you're getting older and much more undesirable. Even with a good resume, a great headshot, and drop-dead good looks, it can take you anywhere from one to three years to get an agent." And if you haven't prepared any alternatives to support yourself, "you'll likely be parking cars or waiting tables to pay the rent."

Perhaps you have connections. You've been introduced. You've met them, had a long meeting, they seemed pleased and interested. Then — nothing. Not another word, and your phone calls are not being returned. What now?

Your natural instinct would be to do something proactive, which in Los Angeles is not easy. In contrast to New York there is very little Equity theatre, which is normally where a good actor could get seen by a good agent. Most of the theatre is actually equity-waiver showcases, where mostly bad actors try to get seen by third-rate agents. And of course, these showcases cost money. Even acting classes are all about getting an agent, and they also cost money. "You're waiting forever for your Big Break," says Mike Pniewski. "Meanwhile the rest of your life just slips away. My priority was my family," he adds. "We needed to find a place to raise kids...and L.A. just wasn't it." Jim Donadio concurs. "We were saving and saving to buy a tiny house we didn't like in a neighborhood we didn't want to live in." At 20-something, this may not be an issue, but at thirty-something, it begins to be a consideration.

I think it's important to be in it for the long haul. Make a life for yourself first. L.A. really has to resonate for you as a place to live.

REBECCA WACKLER, WRITER/DIRECTOR/ACTOR
LOS ANGELES (FORMER ATLANTA RESIDENT)

- **prepare for the competition.** You are used to walking into an audition and seeing the twenty or so people you always see. You are pleasant and maybe even stop to chat afterwards with the ones you know. In L.A. you will be greeted at the casting office by perhaps two hundred people who look *exactly* like you. How can they choose? How could you? You will be competing with thousands of others who have already fought bitterly to get their agent and the auditions they attend, and have survived the most difficult lessons of the business. They're not happy you're here. Don't expect a great deal of help.

"But that's not *me*. I'm *different*."

We have no doubt about it. Just make sure you remember that from now on, whether L.A. ever recognizes it or not .

"But let's suppose what you really want is to act," proposes Kay Hallahan. "and support yourself doing it. Maybe you don't need L.A. You can work right here. Even better, you can make a living being an actor, and soon, not in three years or five years — or never."

The key is inside you. Make it a priority to know yourself as well as you can. Decide what is important to you and why, and what you are willing to risk to attain it. The actions you then take will result from that knowledge, and no matter what happens as a result, there'll be no regrets.

Finale

Let's face it, even when you're extremely talented and make all the right moves this is a tough, tough business. You must have discipline, organization, tenacity, creativity and in the words of actor/author/teacher Uta Hagen, "the unshakable desire to be an actor."

If you've gotten this far and you still think you have the stuff to make it happen, congratulations! We hope we have given you enough ammunition to get you started and keep you going. Drop us a line from time to time. We'd love to hear how you're doing — it lets us know if we've done our job. Just e-mail us at comments@theactorsguide.com.

We applaud your efforts thus far and wish you well in the future, and...break a leg!

Theoretically, the actor ought to be more sound in mind and body than other people, since he learns to understand the psychological problems of human beings when putting his own passions, loves, fears and rages to work in the service of the characters he plays...to do so takes an insatiable curiosity about the human condition.

UTA HAGEN, FROM
A Challenge for the Actor

Notes

Afterword

by George Watkins

As we zoom along in this world of cyberspeak and virtual reality, the parameters that define the truth become blurred and distorted. More and more we witness animated humanoids and cartoon characters dancing across the Web and prancing on the pixels of our video monitors, all during a time when the world is starved for a sense of grounding and authenticity. Never before have we needed emissaries and surrogates to step into the light and help us cobble together sense of meaning and purpose amid labyrinth of chaos and confusion, than we do today. Enter the living, breathing play actor.

Whether you're pitching potato chips or portraying a middle manager in a corporate video, you're still "making movies" and the camera, always the trusty voyeur, seeks out the truth "24 times a second". As you bring your craft to the set, you're joined by an ensemble of gaffers, grips, and cinematographers all poised to realize the writer's vision. There, among the maze of wires and cables, you say your prayers, find your center, and deftly step in the psyche suit of your character.

Feeling the heat of a 12K, you plumb the depths of your emotional palette in an attempt to arrest the moment. Hopefully, if all goes well, you'll be immersed in the eternal NOW, and bring forth a performance that will allow the viewer to smile real smiles, cry real tears, and actually feel the magic and mystery of the human condition. Nothing virtual here. Even as you sell the soap and role-play the part of a corporate automaton you must hold fast to the belief that the world is better off for you having been cast for the part; that it's possible to make a difference, change an attitude… even a life. One might call a profession of this import and magnitude a *calling*.

The audition rooms are filled every day with tentative dilet-tantes holding forth with empty rhetoric that keep the casting tapes running fast forward at warp speed. Enough. We may never really know what primal force drives us to mark our face with paint, dress up, and pretend. Hopefully, it'll remain a deli-cious mystery. But, if deep down in your soul, in that place that knows you choose the thespian path...the way of the player, surrender to it. Give yourself the right and permission to act. At the same time honor the other professionals on the set and pay the price. As an anonymous grip exclaimed on the set, "The pain is temporary, the image eternal." Hear, hear.

Recently, a group of seniors in their seventies and eighties were interviewed about their life's journey. When asked about jobs and careers, they said that their biggest regret was they'd played it too safe. Asked what they'd do differently the second time around, the majority said they'd take more risks. Maybe it's time for you to step up to the mark and bring your light to the world. Who knows? You might even discover yourself along the way.

The camera is rolling.

The Atlanta Journal calls him the "dean of Atlanta directors." Actors call him an actor's director. He's known for his warm, storytelling images, the craft and diplomacy of his work with celebrities, and his ability to evoke strong, sensitive performances even from ordinary folks. He has garnered his share of awards, including a coveted CLIO and the SAG American Scene award. He's directed a little of everything, from live theatre to multi-media shows. At Synergy Films, he continues work as a hands-on director of commercials, documentaries and corporate image projects. When schedule permits, George can also be found lecturing, teaching, and periodically offering an on-camera course. His passion is to bring to the screen REVELATION, a full-length motion picture that's very close to his heart.

As he sees it, after more than three decades in the business, he's really just getting started.

Appendix

Mini Modeling Intro

We'll be frank: we don't know a great deal about modeling and print work — we've never done much of it and it's really not what this book is about. But we get so many inquiries, and indeed there is a great deal of crossover both in the work and in the approach. So we decided to seek some advice and at least provide you will a brief overview. Randall Edwards of Atlanta Models & Talent volunteered us his five-point run-down of the steps involved in researching the print and modeling industry:

1. **First, go to the bookstore or library and find a book on modeling as a career.** "Make sure you get one that's meat & potatoes," Randall emphasizes, "not fluff & stuff." This can give you a more realistic idea of what the work actually entails, and the requirements for specific types of work. Be honest with yourself. You may be fabulously good-looking, but if you're 5" 2" tall you'll almost never qualify to be a fashion model. You may, however, work in commercial print. But is it really a lifestyle that suits you? A substantive book will help you decide.

2. **Become familiar with reputable professionals** in your area who are involved in the industry (**The Actor's Guide Southeast Directory** is a good start). A professional pho-tograher can help you determine your marketability and make suggestions on possible photographs once you begin to assemble your portfolio (**book**). However, you're still at the fact-finding stage: take notes while interviewing three to six photographers for consideration after step 3.

3. **Have a friend take a variety of good snapshots** of you: close-up, full-body, front, back and an active pose or two. "People make the mistake of thinking they have to have a professional composite card to get an evaluation as to whether they are photogenic," says Randall, "when a series of normal, casual photos will serve the purpose very well and are much more cost-effective." Because most agencies have specific preferences in comp cards, if you're signed with one they'll probably then have you create a signature card (a composite card with their agency format and logo) for their use. So first, send your snapshots for evaluation along with a cover letter to several agents in your area. If you don't hear from any of them, follow up if you must, but be prepared to consider another position in the entertainment/advertising/ education field, or another career entirely.

(**Please note:** If you want the photos returned to you, you must provide a SASE. You should not expect to see them again otherwise.)

4. **Interview the various agents that call you back.** Beware of any agents in larger markets that charge fees for pictures, classes or the interview. This is never a prerequisite for representation at a legitimate agency.

5. **Consider training.** There are a few franchised modeling schools that are reputable. However, the quality of the individual schools varies greatly depending on how well each owner maintains their franchise requirements. Thoroughly check and cross-check available model training you're considering. Some professional models have no formal training, so it will depend a great deal on what type of work you seek whether you would necessarily benefit. We must emphasize, however, **that if you do not receive a positive response from your snapshots alone, there is probably no amount of training which can change that.** If you do receive a positive response from a reputable agent, they may then be able to guide you in your training decision.

Remember that by its very nature the modeling profession, like the acting profession, is highly unpredictable. Should you be signed, agents will depend on you for a high-degree of professionalism, availability and flexibilty to pursue the work. Take the time to understand what will be required of you before investing any amount of time and money in such a speculative venture. And remember, if it's too good to be true...

Agency owner Michael Fulmer of Real People Models & Talent in Birmingham tells the story of a 17 year-old woman who came to his office seeking representation as model. Although she was 5' 10" tall, he felt that her look wasn't strong enough to compete professionally even on a local level, so he turned her away. The interview cost her nothing. "It was only on month later when I saw her a large convention in New York. I was surprised, but said hello to her and her mom, and asked her how she came to be there." She said she had attended a modeling school and had been 'selected' to appear before various New York agents. "My heart sank...I knew what had happened. I asked her if any agents had expressed any interest, she told me they had not. I asked her mother how much she had paid for this 'opportunity'. Her reply: about $4000, plus air fare and a week at the hotel."

Glossary

ad-lib – to improvise lines in the context of a scene.

AEA – Actors Equity Association. The union relating to theatre.

agent – see talent agent.

audition – try-out for a commercial, movie, theatre, or television role.

avail/availability – when an agent calls to check an actor's potential scheduling conflicts for a specific time slot prior to booking. It is a courtesy to the producer and indicates interest but is not legally binding.

AFTRA – American Federation of Television and Radio Artists.

booking – being hired for a job.

booking out – informing your talent agency ahead of time when you are going out of town or unavailable to audition for an extended period of time.

breakdown – List of roles and descriptions provided to agents by producers or casting directors. Normally refers that published by Breakdown Services, Ltd., but can also be used to refer to the list provided by an individual producer or director. Usually this list includes; a character description of roles being cast, story line, shoot dates, production company, and whether the project is union or non-union.

broadcast – program tranmission from radio or television station.

buy-out – In lieu of residuals, a set fee negotiated for a specific period of time in which a client is permitted to broadcast a commercial spot.

cap – for a buy-out, the time limit a spot is allowed to broadcast.

call-back – an additional audition for the same project.

call sheet – a daily listing of call times for cast and crew.

call time – the time you are supposed to be on the set, ready to work.

casting director – the person hired by the producer to secure talent.

cattle call – a derogatory term used for an unrestricted or open audition.

chops – a slang term for acting experience and ability.

cold reading – When an actor reads a script without having rehearsed.

commercial – an on-camera advertisement for a product.

commission – The set percentage of an actor's payment due to an agent for his service. Customarily commissions are 15% for non-union work, 10% for union.

comp/composite card – generally a 5x7 card with numerous color pictures used to solicit print work.

conflict – (commercial) when you've been hired by one advertiser (and have a commercial airing) which in turn prevents you from working for any of their competitors. Compensation is in the form of a Holding Fee.

contact sheet – or proof sheet. A page of film-sized pictures, each of which contains an entire film roll of shots from your photo shoot.

copy – an on-camera or voice-over commercial script.

day player – for film or television, an actor employed by the day.

deal – the negotiated agreement between the talent and the hiring authority for any production.

demo tape/reel – a video or audio sample of representative selections from an actor's body of work, either on-camera or voice-over. Class work is not acceptable for demo tapes.

dialogue – a script for two or more characters.

director – one who coordinates the technical and creative aspects of a production.

downgrade – when a role has been diminished in the final product either being eliminated or made unrecognizable.

ear prompter – a device fit into an actor's ear, which allows them to hear pre-recorded or live information.

8 x 10 – the traditional black and white headshot. Color is becoming acceptable, but is never required.

exclusivity – having one agent represent you in a given department.

executive producer – person who funds the project.

extra – background talent.

first refusal – this is not a booking, but a courtesy to casting. talent agrees to notify the client should another offer come in for the same date and time; not legally binding.

franchised agent – an agent approved by the union to find talent and negotiate on their behalf.

freelance – to sign with more than one agent.

go see – an audition for a print job.

hand model – a talent whose hands are used for a production.

headshot – a black and white 8x10 picture of you that the agent uses to market an actor.

hold – a legally binding agreement between talent and producer to hold a specific day open for the job.

holding fee – the fixed fee paid every thirteen weeks to keep a commercial active.

improvisation/improv – to perform, create, sing or recite extemporaneously, without preparation.

industrial – a corporate or non-broadcast film or video.

laser reproduction – reproducing a headshot digitally, using toner for printing. The quality is compromised so this is recommended for short run printing and is generally used for comp cards.

lift – taking one part of a commercial to re-use in another commercial.

lithographic reproduction – high quality dot printing made by a printing press. It's recommended for mass quantity reproduction. This is cheaper than photographic because it uses ink and a less expensive grade of paper. While this isn't the highest quality, it's acceptable, and generally the norm, in secondary markets.

looping – recording voice-over in a film, done once the film has wrapped.

loupe – a magnifying eyeglass used for reviewing film-sized prints on contact sheets.

mark – the spot on the floor indicating where an actor should stand.

monologue – a narrative script performed by one actor.

MOW – movie of the week.

national – a commercial which airs throughout the country.

non-broadcast – a project which is not aired on network or cable television.

OC/off-camera – action or dialog not seen on the screen.

open call – an audition open to the general public.

PA – production assistant, assistant to the producer on the set.

per diem – designated fee paid by the production company on union projects for daily expenses on an out-of-town.

photo double – an actor performing in place of another; usually only seen from behind.

photographic reproduction – produced chemically through a photographic process on high quality, photographic paper. Although this is more expensive, the major markets generally prefer photographic to lithographic.

preference – when an actor declares to a specified casting director that he 'prefers' to be called through one specific agency.

principal – a performer with lines or special business which advances the story.

producer – the decision maker and sometimes money-controller on a project.

proofs – contact sheet.

prop – any object used on a set in a scene.

PSA – Public Service Announcement.

reel – see demo tape.

regional commercial – a commercial that airs in a select area.

release – written permission giving the producer rights to use an actor's work or likeness for a certain amount of time.

residual – compensation paid to a performer for the re-use of a film, commercial, or television project.

resume – a written summary of an actor's experience in the entertainment industry, which is attached to the back of the headshot.

right-to-work – the low that secures the right of employees to decide for themselves whether or not to join or financially support a union.

right-to-work states – Alabama, Arizona, Arkansas, Florida, Georgia, Idaho, Iowa, Kansas, Louisiana, Mississippi, Nebraska, Nevada, North Carolina, North Dakota, South Carolina, South Dakota, Tennessee, Texas, Utah, Virginia, Wyoming.

SAG – Screen Actors Guild.

SAG-eligible – an actor becomes eligible to join the union after working as a principal one union job or as an extra in three union commercials.

Scale – the minimum wage set by the union.

Scale + 10 – the minimum wage plus the ten percent to cover the agent commission.

session fee – payment for the initial performance in a commercial.

set – the site or location of the shoot.

sides – parts or scenes from a film or television script used in an audition. The word sides originated when casting directors would get parts of the script for auditions. They would put them "aside" and began calling them sides.

signatory – an employer who produces under the terms of a union contract.

sign-in – recording your name, social security number, agency and audition time on the sheet at a union audition.

spokesperson – a principal actor hired in a commercial or non-broadcast video to represent the company, product or service being promoted or presented.

spot – a :15 to :60 broadcast advertisement for a product or service.

slate – the verbal identification by the performer before an audition; Also, a small chalkboard or clapboard device used to identify scene and take

stand-in – an extra who stands in place of the principal performer for the purpose of setting lights or any other technical aspects.

storyboard – the synopsis of a commercial illustrated by representative frames of action and dialogue in sequential order.

submission – the agent's suggestions of actors to a casting director for a particular role in a project.

Taft–Hartley – a 30 day grace period after first union employment before being required to join a union.

TelePrompTer – a device which displays and scrolls the script as it's being read by the actor, avoiding the necessity of memorizing the copy. When positioned next to the camera, it appears the actor is looking directly into the lens.

theatrical – TV or film work.

trades – publications geared toward the entertainment industry.

trailer – clips from a film used for promotional purposes.

turnaround – when shooting multiple days, the amount of time from dismissal at end-of-day to call time the next day.

under-5 – a principal role having five lines or less (AFTRA).

understudy – a performer who studies and prepares to take the place of the principal performer should the need arise. A theater term only.

union – the organization that negotiates and polices the regulations and conditions under which actors work.

upgrade – when an actor who was booked as an extra is featured in the finished product and is later paid as a principal.

use cycle – 13-week period during which a commercial is aired; used to determine payment schedule.

voice-over – the voice of an off-camera actor, narrator or spokesperson.

voucher – a agency contract for print or non-union work.

wardrobe – required clothing for a shoot.

wardrobe fitting – a paid session to fit your costume for a (union) shoot.

wild spot – commercial contracted to air on a station-by-station basis rather than by network.

Audition Cheat Sheet

Date & Time of Audition: Agency:

Project Name:

Role: Union/Non-union:

Audition Location/Address:

Contact(s):

Sides available:

Wardrobe requirements:

Special Instructions:

Shoot Dates: Callback Dates:

Location of Shoot:

Commercial Conflicts:

Directions to Location:

Alternate Directions:

Estimated Driving Time:

Beg Mileage: Ending Mileage:

Parking Fees: 1st Audition or Callback:

(Adapted from **Bren's Cheat Sheet** in **The Actor's Guide for Kids**)

Job Cheat Sheet

Type of Project: Commercial   Feature Film   Episodic   MOW
                    Industrial   Voice-over   Print   Other

Project Name:

Role: Union/Non-Union:

Date(s) of booking:

Talent Agency: Casting Director:

Wardrobe/fittings:

Production Co./Studio:

Ad Agency: Network:

Director: Producer:

Call Time: Contact:

Location: Local or OOT:

Directions:

Compensation:Billing:

Exclusivity/Commercial   Conflicts:

Travel & Living Compensation: Per Diem   Hotel   Mileage   Airfare

Dressing Facility: Trailer:

Who do I contact for a copy of the project?

When?

DON"T FORGET: Voucher/Contract   ID   Script

(Adapted from Jen's Cheat Sheet in **The Actor's Guide for Kids**)

Typical Players: Film & Television Production

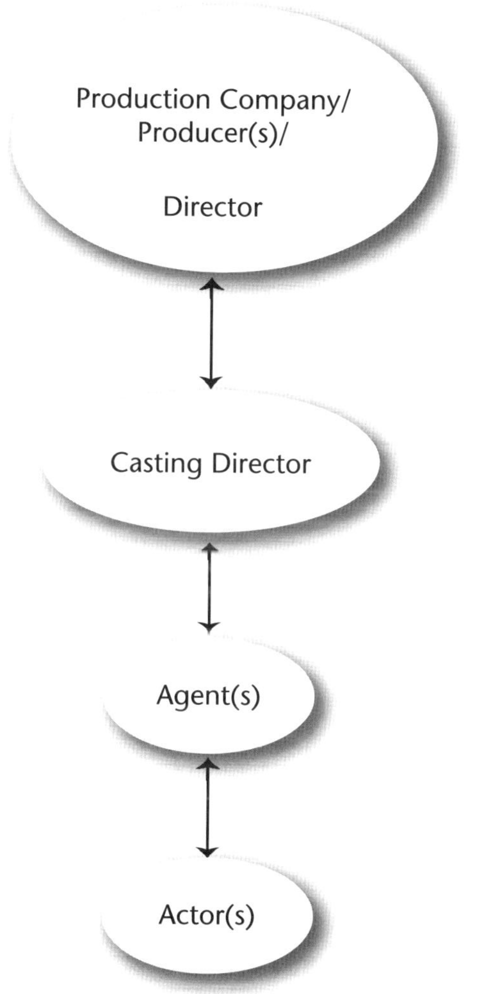

The number of individuals involved in casting will depend on the overall size of the production itself. In smaller independents, the writer/producer/director and even lead actor may all be the same person.

Typical Players: Commercial Production

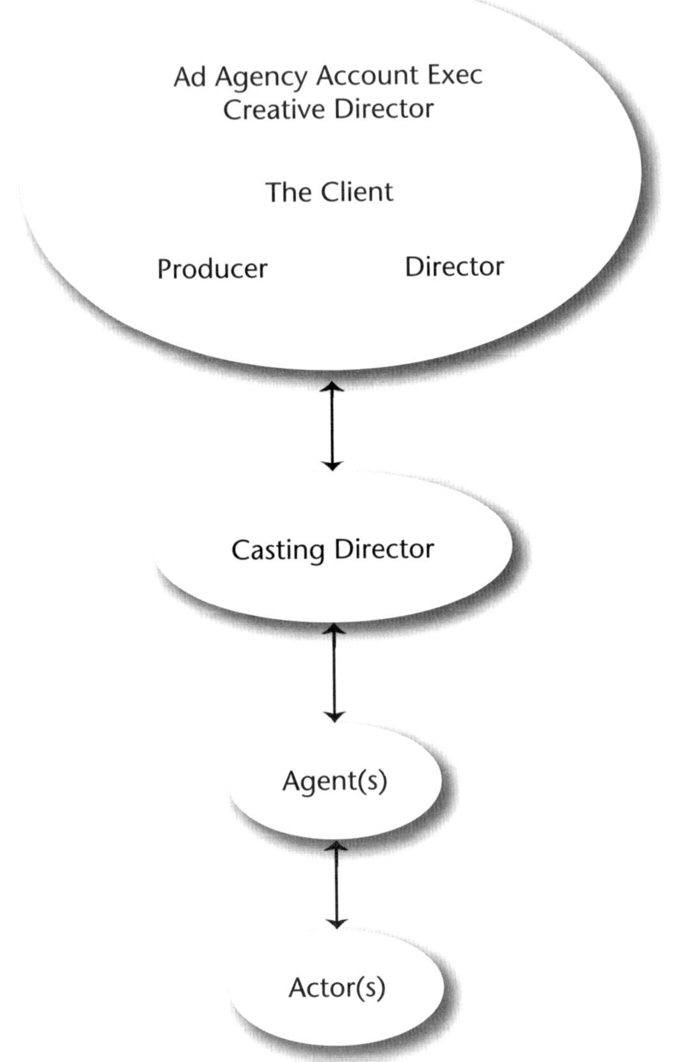

Add in a copywriter, several more agents and who knows how many actors, you can easily see how involved the casting process for a big budget commercial can be.